New York Theater Walks

New York Theater Walks

Seven Historical Tours from Times Square to Greenwich Village and Beyond

Howard Kissel

Photographs by Brent Brolin

APPLAUSE THEATRE & CINEMA BOOKS
An Imprint of Hal Leonard Corporation
New York

Published in a 2007 by Applause Theatre & Cinema Books
An Imprint of Hal Leonard Corporation
19 West 21st Street, New York, NY 10010

Printed in the United States of America

Book design by Kristi Montague

Maps by Kevin Hein

Library of Congress Cataloging-in-Publication Data

Kissel, Howard.
  New York theater walks : seven historical tours from Times Square to Greenwich Village and beyond / Howard Kissel.
    p. cm.
  Includes index.
  ISBN 978-1-55783-613-7
  1. Theater—New York (State)—New York—Guidebooks.
  2. Theaters—New York (State)—New York—Guidebooks.
  3. Walking—New York (State)—New York—Guidebooks. I. Title.
PN2277.N5K57 2007
792.09747'1—dc22
                              2007036786

www.applausepub.com

This is the first of my books that will go to press without benefit of the editorial wisdom of my wife, Christine, who died in the summer of 2006. Every corner of the city, which we explored during our early years together, carries some memory of her. I dedicate this book to her warm, inspiring spirit.

CONTENTS

INTRODUCTION

Unlike many of America's first cities, New York was not founded under religious auspices. It was developed by the Dutch purely as a commercial venture, and from its earliest years it had a reputation for two things—it was a place people went to make money and to have a good time.

That is why theater is embedded in New York's streets and sidewalks. While many American cities turned to building cultural centers in the mid-20th century—often in areas blighted by urban decay—as a way of reviving their fortunes, New York (though boasting its own urban renewal success story in the Lincoln Center for the Performing Arts) was built as much upon show business as upon finance. Until the early 20th century, when the Interborough Rapid Transit built a subway station at what had been Longacre Square, heralding the rise of the Broadway theater district, New York theater had worked its way uptown alongside the city itself.

Of course, theater was also a part of the economy of other American cities. Before motion pictures and television, theater was a far more national art than it is today. Joseph Jefferson and Minnie Maddern Fiske, two of the greatest stars of the 19th century, did not achieve stardom by making a few appearances on Leno or Letterman. They were regular visitors to every city in the country. When you consider the state of the highways before the invention of the automobile you have a sense of how grueling the road to fame was.

Every city of any size had several theaters with a certain number of drop curtains. Traveling theatrical companies put on plays that made use of those sets so that they would not have to schlep scenery in addition to the costumes that were as much a part of each actor's stock in trade as the Shakespearean (and lesser) roles that he or she had memorized. Several cities had storage buildings constructed so that actors could rent space to keep the costumes they would not need for a specific itinerary.

By the early 20th century, however, movies were quickly replacing the theater as the primary national entertainment. Suspenseful movies like *The Perils of Pauline* were also taking over the business of providing melodramatic thrills that the theater had provided in the late 19th century in such popular favorites as *Bertha the Sewing Machine Girl*, the key scene of which showed Bertha tied to a plank in a lumber mill moving toward the deadly circular saw. Theater could not compete with the realism of movies, and so it moved toward the psychological and intellectual concerns exemplified by the plays of Eugene O'Neill.

It was in New York that theater continued to thrive most strongly despite the competition of new forms. Moreover, by the mid-20th century theater was no longer focused only on Broadway. Tiny groups, similar to the Provincetown Playhouse, which had fostered O'Neill, were springing up in neighborhoods where real estate was cheap, first in the West Village, then in the East Village. This proliferation of theaters continues—in the early years of the 21st century, theaters are being built in the hitherto forgotten regions of the West '30s.

All of this is by way of explaining that only one of the walking tours in this book focuses exclusively on Times Square. Nor does that tour explain, theater by theater, when each was built and what plays have been presented there. (Several books—notably Mary Henderson's *The City* and the Theater and Louis Botto's *At This Theater*—have done that quite comprehensively.) Instead, these tours reflect the fact that theater has pervaded the whole city.

This book has been written for visitors to New York, giving them an introduction to neighborhoods not necessarily on the beaten path, but I hope it will also be useful to people who live here, who often take the history and wonders that surround us for granted.

WALK ONE

THE BROADWAY
THEATER DISTRICT

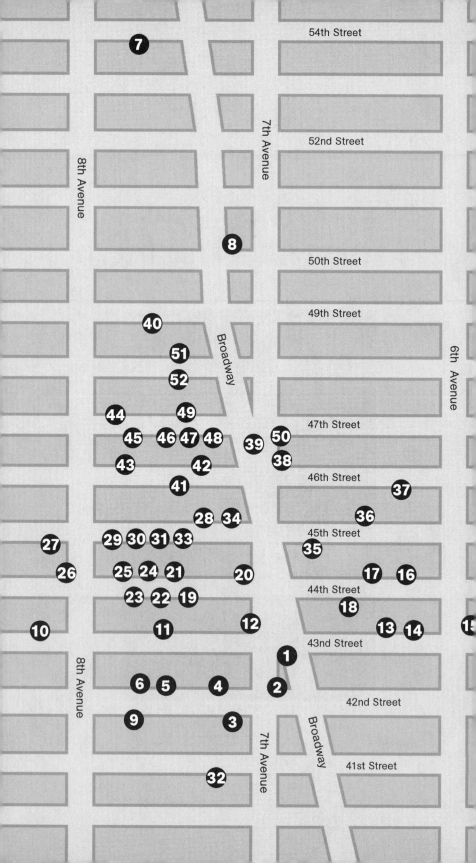

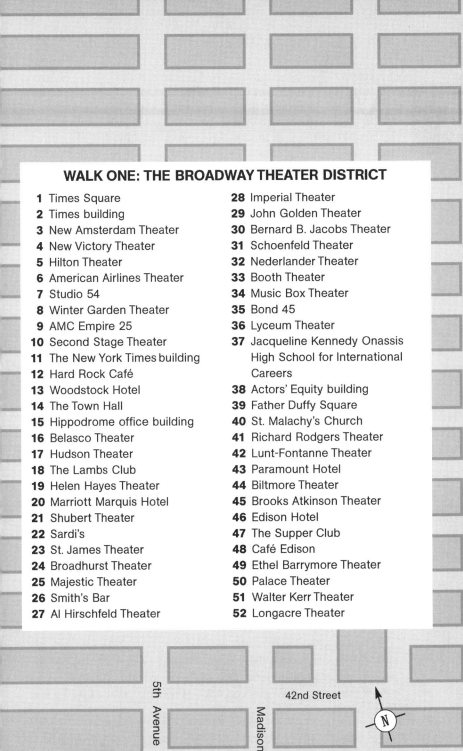

WALK ONE: THE BROADWAY THEATER DISTRICT

1 Times Square
2 Times building
3 New Amsterdam Theater
4 New Victory Theater
5 Hilton Theater
6 American Airlines Theater
7 Studio 54
8 Winter Garden Theater
9 AMC Empire 25
10 Second Stage Theater
11 The New York Times building
12 Hard Rock Café
13 Woodstock Hotel
14 The Town Hall
15 Hippodrome office building
16 Belasco Theater
17 Hudson Theater
18 The Lambs Club
19 Helen Hayes Theater
20 Marriott Marquis Hotel
21 Shubert Theater
22 Sardi's
23 St. James Theater
24 Broadhurst Theater
25 Majestic Theater
26 Smith's Bar
27 Al Hirschfeld Theater

28 Imperial Theater
29 John Golden Theater
30 Bernard B. Jacobs Theater
31 Schoenfeld Theater
32 Nederlander Theater
33 Booth Theater
34 Music Box Theater
35 Bond 45
36 Lyceum Theater
37 Jacqueline Kennedy Onassis High School for International Careers
38 Actors' Equity building
39 Father Duffy Square
40 St. Malachy's Church
41 Richard Rodgers Theater
42 Lunt-Fontanne Theater
43 Paramount Hotel
44 Biltmore Theater
45 Brooks Atkinson Theater
46 Edison Hotel
47 The Supper Club
48 Café Edison
49 Ethel Barrymore Theater
50 Palace Theater
51 Walter Kerr Theater
52 Longacre Theater

5th Avenue

Madison Avenue

42nd Street

N

1

Most of the walks we will take together will require the use of the imagination. This quality, which as a theater lover you presumably have in abundant supply, is important in New York because the city changes so rapidly. A 19th-century anecdote has it that a distinguished visitor was greeted downtown at City Hall and given a tour of the city on his way up to lunch. On his journey back down to City Hall he was shown all the changes that had taken place while he had eaten.

Even in the course of preparing this book, certain buildings that seem to have been in place forever have been destroyed. Only two days after finishing this chapter, I was startled to read that the Lambs Club, which had been the subject of negotiation between preservationists and developers, would finally be torn down. I have left the description in place in the—I'm afraid—naïve hope that yet another compromise may be effected.

While many of the walks in this book feature buildings that you will have to imagine, on this walk we will concentrate on what has been here for a long time.

It must be remembered, of course, that **Times Square** itself is only a little over a century old. Before the turn of the 20th century this area was known as Longacre Square, and, like the Long Acre district in London, it was home to stables, blacksmiths, and horse markets. It was, in effect, suburban, but two things were changing its status: the automobile and the subway, both of which brought this area of the city within the reach of people who lived further downtown and did not own horses or buggies.

What drew these visitors northward? Times Square was developed primarily as a pleasure center. Although there were theaters and music halls throughout the city, certain areas of town grew in connection with specific industries, like the garment center just to the south. The industry that created the neighborhood we are about to walk through was entertainment. Journalism, then as now, is a branch of the entertainment industry, and it was the arrival of the offices of the *New York Times* that gave the neighborhood its name.

Let's begin our walk on the southeast corner of Seventh Avenue and 42nd Street, where there is an entrance to the subway appropriately decked out in neon. Originally the station underneath was a spur from Grand Central on the subway line that came up the East Side.

The *Times* opened its new building on December 31, 1904, with a display of fireworks, which inaugurated the idea that this was *the* place to celebrate New Year's Eve. We're standing on 42nd Street on the downtown side of the street, looking across at the

Times Square

triangular **Times building**. It echoes the Flatiron Building at 23rd Street, where Broadway intersects with Fifth Avenue. We can't really judge the architectural merits of the tower since its surface has been altered many times in the past 100 years.

Before beginning our walk, let's look back at the huge office building on the southeast corner of Broadway and 42nd Street. When it was built, in 1902, it was the Knickerbocker Hotel and was home to such distinguished tenants as Enrico Caruso, who worked a few blocks down Broadway when the Metropolitan Opera was there, as well as George M. Cohan, who performed in several of the theaters that were soon to be built to the north. The hotel served a very fashionable clientele, and the equally fashionable painter Maxfield Parrish was commissioned to do a painting of Old King Cole for its bar. The hotel was converted to an office building before World War II and the painting was moved uptown to the St. Regis Hotel, where it has long been the centerpiece of one of its restaurants.

Now let's walk west on 42nd Street. It is hard to imagine that this now resplendent block was, during the last few decades of the 20th century, a sewer. The movie theaters on both sides of the street showed only pornography. Many buildings had been condemned, but there were no plans to replace them. Various city commissions had proposed ways to overhaul the moribund block—the plans invariably featured a trolley car, as if the kind of conveyance featured on Disneyland's Main Street, U.S.A., would transform the sordid surroundings into a congenial environment.

1

Disney would in fact play a role in the street's renaissance, but it was another very un-New York institution, the Gap, that sparked the transformation. The opening of a Gap store in Times Square signified to the 42nd Street Development Project that there was now a strong enough suburban middle-class tourist presence in the city to persuade investors to revitalize this seemingly hopeless street. In the mid-'90s, the Walt Disney Corporation invested

$36 million (with comparable funding from New York City and State) to renovate one of the most beautiful buildings on the street, which we're approaching now—the **New Amsterdam Theater**, designed by the firm of Herts and Tallent, which opened in 1903.

In a way it was a blessing that, like Sleeping Beauty, the New Amsterdam had been dormant for so long (it had been shut down as a movie theater in 1979). Had it been renovated earlier, it might have been modernized, but by the mid-'90s the value of New York's architectural heritage was recognized, and the firm of Hardy Holzman Pfeiffer Associates, which specialized in historical renovation, was hired to restore the theater to its former glory. Disney was probably the ideal producer for this theater, for its décor reflects the same turn-of-the-century fairy-tale esthetic that underlies Disney's early animated features.

New Amsterdam Theater

From its inception, the New Amsterdam was full of European touches, with a rich sense of fantasy in its art nouveau décor. Fittingly, the first production it held was *A Midsummer Night's Dream*. For the first nine years after its renovation, Disney's *The Lion King*, which opened in October 1997, was the attraction, and for the next umpteen it will be the stage version of Disney's *Mary Poppins*. The New Amsterdam is one of the only Broadway theaters that gives regular guided tours of its interior.

Across the street is the **New Victory Theater**. It was one of the first theaters to go up on this block, dating from 1902, when it

New Victory Theater

was built by Oscar Hammerstein. Hammerstein was also building much more lavish entertainment centers around the corner, like the Olympia, a huge building that combined theaters and restaurants at Broadway and 44th Street. By contrast, this theater, then named the Republic, was an intimate space for serious plays. Hammerstein called it "the perfect parlor theater." Its first production starred Lionel Barrymore.

Not all of its attractions were serious. In 1923 *Abie's Irish Rose* opened here and, to the dismay of critics and high-minded theatergoers, became one of Broadway's longest-running hits. (A mere two years later Lorenz Hart, in his lyrics for "Manhattan," wrote, "Our future babies / We'll take to *Abie's / Irish Rose. /* I hope they'll live to see it close." It seems worth noting that 80 years ago two years was considered a long run.) In 1932 the theater was bought by Billy Minsky and became the neighborhood's first burlesque house. Minsky created a tacky façade that was equally appropriate in the '70s, when it became the city's first XXX-rated porno theater.

Interestingly, it was the first theater to be renovated as the new 42nd Street took shape. When it reopened in December 1995, the stunningly restored Venetian exterior with its period lamps and grand staircase almost seemed a mirage on a street that was then largely desolate. Renamed the New Victory Theater, it presents sophisticated children's theater and dance.

Next to the New Victory is the **Hilton**, another renovated theater, intended as a house for musicals, which respectfully incorpo-

1

rated elements of the interiors of two of the earliest theaters on 42ⁿᵈ Street: the Lyric, whose ornate façade we will see around the corner on 43ʳᵈ Street, and the Apollo, which was the first Shubert Theater in New York. Both these theaters had long been movie houses—in the '50s and '60s, 42ⁿᵈ Street was a place where you could see second-run movies, at a lower cost than when they were new. By the '80s most of these cinemas were showing porno, though the Apollo held out for a long time as a place that showed "serious" films.

The first show to open in the Hilton, which was originally called the Ford Center, was *Ragtime*, a musical version of E.L. Doctorow's novel with book by Terrence McNally and score by Lynn Ahrens and Stephen Flaherty. It starred Marin Mazzie and Brian Stokes Mitchell. The musical, like the theater itself, was the brainchild of a Canadian entrepreneur named Garth Drabinsky, whose bookkeeping practices led to numerous indictments under New York state law that have kept him in Canada. Without his chutzpah, however, this handsomely proportioned theater might not exist.

The **American Airlines Theater** is an elegantly restored version of the Selwyn, named for the Selwyns, who were busy producers in the early part of the 20ᵗʰ century. It is one of several theaters belonging to the Roundabout Theater Company, which began its life in the late '60s in the basement of a supermarket on West 26ᵗʰ Street. Like many Off-Off-Broadway companies that were founded back then, it was devoted to revivals of classical plays. Over the years the Roundabout has occasionally presented new work, but it still focuses on revivals here and at **Studio 54** a dozen blocks uptown.

Although many people in the theater resent the presence of corporate names on theaters (the venerable **Winter Garden** up at 50ᵗʰ Street was for a time the Cadillac Winter Garden), the willingness of huge corporations to lend their names to Broad-

Second Stage Theater

8

1

way houses is perhaps the most amazing sign of the rebirth of the neighborhood. Until fairly recently no shareholder would have wanted his or her company associated with the theater district.

As we walk west on 42nd Street it seems worth noting the great effort made to retain the visual honky-tonk effect always associated with Times Square. Most of the buildings we're passing are new, but on the south side of the street close to Eighth Avenue is a huge, ornate movie complex called the **AMC Empire 25**. It is a measure of the care that went into planning the restoration of the block that the façade of the Empire, though hardly a design of architectural distinction, was transported about 100 feet west so that some of the original feeling of the street could be preserved. The Empire façade is a reminder of the grandeur that used to be associated with movie palaces.

Let's turn right and walk up Eighth Avenue. On the northwest corner of 43rd Street is an Off-Broadway theater called **Second Stage**, which started in the '70s as a company devoted to reviving neglected contemporary plays rather than classics. It still does, though it also produces new work. Its original home was on the top floor of a seedy hotel just off Central Park West behind the Dakota. It then moved to an-

The 2007 home of the *New York Times*

other high floor in a building on upper Broadway, but its current home reflects the sophisticated attitude toward architecture of the new century. Second Stage hired the eminent Dutch architect Rem Koolhaus to create its new theater space inside the splendid art deco shell of a defunct bank.

As we walk east on 43rd Street we see what were the offices of the *New York Times*, which moved here when it outgrew the triangular building around the corner. The newspaper is now headquartered in a huge skyscraper at Eighth Avenue and 41st Street.

As we make the first of our crossings of Broadway, it seems worth noting the variety and size of the signs that abound. The birth

**The Paramount building, whose marquee
now advertises the Hard Rock Café**

of Times Square coincided with the birth of electrical signage. In 1916 the city passed a zoning ordinance encouraging huge signs. When George Bernard Shaw was brought here he remarked, "It must be wonderful for people who can't read."

Standing on an island in the middle of traffic, let's look back at the distinctive marquee that was created for the Paramount Theater, which now advertises the **Hard Rock Café**. The Paramount was built in 1926, a year before the introduction of sound in motion pictures. Its opulence was such that—allegedly—people paid the admission fee simply to walk around its lavish interiors without necessarily bothering to watch the film. The interior of the theater itself was ten stories high. When Radio City Music Hall was built six years later, it was deliberately designed to eclipse the wonders of the Paramount and another showplace nearby, the Roxy, which was demolished in the '60s. It was a photograph of Gloria Swanson

10

standing in the ruins of the Roxy that inspired the Stephen Sondheim musical *Follies.*

Movie theaters in the '20s were competing with vaudeville. They didn't just give you a movie; there was also live entertainment. The Paramount, of course, is remembered as the place where the young Frank Sinatra rendered bobbie soxers hysterical during World War II. Because of the high cost of real estate in the inflationary '20s, the building was originally designed to have offices in addition to the theater. By the '50s the towering space that had been the Paramount was more valuable as offices than as an entertainment center.

Let's finish crossing the street. As we walk along 43rd Street, we see the newly sandblasted exterior of the **Woodstock Hotel**, which is typical of the apartment hotels that proliferated in this neighborhood in the last decades of the 19th century and the early decades of the 20th. They were designed for people climbing the social ladder who could not yet afford to build mansions, let alone pay for the sizeable staff necessary to maintain them. They could stay in such hotels until they amassed enough capital to build their own homes further uptown. By the 1980s, when the neighborhood had reached its nadir, the Woodstock had become federally subsidized housing for the elderly and infirm.

It made headlines in 1999 when a gigantic scaffold being used to construct the Condé-Nast building around the corner collapsed and fell on top of it, crushing a woman who lived on its top floor. A few years later the Woodstock was acquired by a developer and turned into condominiums.

As we approach Sixth Avenue we see the stately Georgian façade of the **Town Hall**, which was designed by the eminent firm of McKim, Mead & White. The money for the building was donated by a member of the Bliss family (who were also major contributors to the Metropolitan Opera) on behalf of the League for Political Education. The League had been founded in 1894 when an amendment to the New York State Constitution to permit women to vote was defeated.

Unlike most of the buildings in this neighborhood, which were geared for show business, this one was intended to raise the level of political discourse. By the time it was finished, in 1921, women's suffrage had been achieved. Nevertheless, its civic usefulness continues to this day. Its intimate interior is perfect for lectures and debates, and its excellent acoustics make it a great concert hall.

At the beginning of this walk I said we would not need to use our imaginations. Here we have a choice. As we turn the corner onto Sixth Avenue, we can look across at the office building called

11

1

the **Hippodrome** and imagine what it was like when it was a huge entertainment complex that housed a menagerie in its basement and a stage complete with a water tank for aquatic ballets. Or we can go across the street, pop our heads into the otherwise Spartan lobby, and see photographs of the lost splendors of this most ambitious of New York theaters.

As we turn west on 44th Street, we see the **Belasco**, built in 1907 and named for the innovative producer David Belasco. He was most famous for his daring stage effects and lighting, though he also created plays that have found enduring life in two operas by Giacomo Puccini: *Madame Butterfly* and *The Girl of the Golden*

West. Belasco, who dressed in priestly garb, though hardly because he had a priestly outlook on life, had an apartment in his theater with a peephole that allowed him to keep an eye on what was going on onstage. The interior has a lot of lights behind stained glass, an innovation at the time since it obviated the need for chandeliers, which might restrict the audience's view. Supposedly Belasco's ghost still inhabits the theater.

A little way down 44th Street is the 1903 **Hudson Theater**, which is now part of the Millennium Hotel. It has not been used much as a theater for many years, but is now mainly used for corporate events. This is a pity, because it means people seldom have the opportunity to see its beautiful Tiffany mosaic

Hudson Theater

tiles. Just as the Republic (now the New Victory) opened with Lionel Barrymore, the Hudson's first production, *Cousin Kate*, starred his sister, Ethel.

Across the street is one of the most charming and intimate theaters in the neighborhood, on an upper story of the **Lambs Club**. The Lambs originated in London in the mid-19th century, as a theatrical and dining club named in honor of Charles and Mary Lamb. Its members were show people. The same was true of the American version, and the roster of former members, starting with, say, Fred Astaire, is extremely impressive. Like another fraternal showbiz organization, the Friars, which still pays mocking tribute to members in its Roasts, the Lambs had their Gambols. Their original function as a convivial club has been supplemented by philanthropic activities. The theater was even scheduled for demolition, but a last-

1

minute compromise was effected so the theater will remain within yet another office complex.

Let's cross Broadway again. Looking down toward the stretch of 44th Street closest to Eighth Avenue, we see one of the busiest corners in the neighborhood, a reminder of what a bustling area this was before the clusters of theaters and restaurants were broken up by huge high-rises. Each of these theaters is splendidly designed, and all have been beautifully restored.

As early as 1912, people were rebelling against the commercialism that characterized most of the theater. A result of this rebellion was the theater now called the **Helen Hayes**, which began its life as the Little Theater. It was indeed little, holding only 299 seats. And it was intended to provide a proper house for plays that required an intimate audience. It was renamed for the beloved actress in 1983, when the theater that had long borne her name was demolished to make room for the **Marriott Marquis Hotel**. Its current incarnation includes 597 seats.

One of the most beloved theaters on Broadway, the **Shubert**, built in 1913, was named for the family that constructed many of the theaters in this neighbor-

Helen Hayes Theater

Cows, Coconuts, Killer Rabbits, Witches, and French People.

Shubert Theater

13

St. James Theater

1

hood as well as a chain of theaters across the country. The Shuberts were born in Syracuse, New York, but arrived in New York before World War I, when this neighborhood was a boom town. (*The Boys from Syracuse*, the title of the Richard Rodgers–Lorenz Hart adaptation of Shakespeare's *A Comedy of Errors*, was an affectionate tribute to the brothers Lee and J. J. Shubert.) This theater was named for their older brother Sam, who founded the business and was killed at the age of 29 in a train crash.

The Shuberts still maintain their offices above the theater. During the dark days of the Depression they were generous to producers who wanted to rent their theaters, not out of innate altruism but simply as a way of keeping the neighborhood—and their business—alive. The Shubert's longest running tenant was *A Chorus Line*, which occupied the house for 15 years.

One of the things that turned **Sardi's**, an unassuming mom-and-pop Italian restaurant, into one of the city's most long-lasting and popular landmarks was its proximity to the Shuberts' offices, the nerve center of Broadway. Another thing, of course, was the tastiness of its signature dishes. Caricatures of its celebrity clientele have hung on its walls for many decades. Vincent Sardi first opened his restaurant down the block, where the St. James theater now stands, in 1921, but it has been here since 1927.

The **Broadhurst**, next door to the Shubert, was named for a British playwright who arrived here in the late 19th century and

Broadhurst Theater

1

had an active career not just writing plays but managing theaters all across the country. He opened the theater in 1917 with the New York premiere of *Misalliance*, a play by his fellow countryman George Bernard Shaw. The proportions of the Broadhurst make it an excellent theater for serious drama.

By contrast, the **Majestic** next door, whose interior certainly lives up to its name, is a perfect house for musicals. Ever since 1988 it has been the home of Andrew Lloyd-Webber's *The Phantom of the Opera*, and there is a good chance, even if you buy this book secondhand decades from now, that will still be the case.

Across the street is another house that also mostly plays host to musicals, the **St. James**. Its distinctive exterior, featuring what looks like an elaborate birdcage, was inspired by the architecture of Georgian London. At one point, in the mid-'40s, the St. James and the Majestic, both finished in 1927, had Rodgers and Hammerstein's first two masterpieces running simultaneously—*Oklahoma!* at the St. James and *Carousel* at the Majestic. One of its long-running recent tenants was a theatrical adaptation of *The Who's Tommy*.

As we again approach Eighth Avenue, let's glance across the street at **Smith's Bar**, a dimly lit place that serves basic food and alcohol at very reasonable prices. Its frowzy ambience is a reminder that the theater once shared this neighborhood with the world of boxing. Madison Square Garden was up the street at 49th, and the intervening blocks were filled with similar bars, as well as pool halls and training gyms. The neighborhood was also dominated by steak joints that catered to the Garden's patrons, unlike the more culinarily adventurous establishments that now feed theatergoers.

Smith's Bar

Before turning east on 45th Street, let's look across Eighth Avenue and notice the witty façade of the **Al Hirschfeld Theater**, named for the beloved artist whose uniquely vivid and enduring caricatures of Broadway shows began running in New York newspapers in 1926, when he was 23. The theater was dedicated in June 2003 on what would have been Hirschfeld's 100th birthday.

Although in ostensible good health, he died quietly about six months before his birthday.

Al Hirschfeld Theater

The theater itself, which has a Moorish aspect both outside and in, opened in 1924. It was named for the man who built it, Martin Beck, who also built the Palace. When Rocco Landesman, the head of Jujamcyn Theaters, which owns it, decided it should be renamed the Hirschfeld, his hardest task, he said, was informing Beck's heirs of his decision. Their response was entirely gracious.

Inside the theater is a gallery of original Hirschfelds illustrating plays and musicals that appeared in this theater, including the original 1946 production of Eugene O'Neill's *The Iceman Cometh* and the 1977 production of *Dracula* that starred Frank Langella.

Turning east, we see a stretch as dense as 44th Street in terms of the number of theaters. The uptown side of the street used to be equally dense with restaurants, including one of the last remaining places that had begun as a speakeasy, but in the prosperity of the first years of the 21st century they were all demolished to make way for yet another high-rise apartment building.

With the exception of the **Imperial**, a grand place for musicals, all of the theaters on this stretch are fairly intimate, making them perfect settings for plays and comedies. The first of them, named for the producer **John Golden**, has often been used for small-cast shows, like *An Evening with Mike Nichols and Elaine May*, which introduced those Second City talents to New York in 1960, or *Beyond the Fringe*, which introduced the Brits Alan Bennett, Peter

1

Imperial Theater

Cook, Jonathan Miller, and Dudley Moore to America a few years later. It has also housed intimate musicals like *Avenue Q.*

In the summer of 2005, two of the handful of theaters not named for anyone, which for decades had been known as the Royale and the Plymouth, were renamed for **Bernard B. Jacobs** and **Gerald**

Schoenfeld, who since the early '70s had run the Shubert Organization. Not everyone in the theater community was enthusiastic about naming theaters for hard-nosed businessmen rather than actresses or playwrights, but it was noted that the **Nederlander**, on 41st Street, where *Rent* opened in 1996, has long been named for the founder of the dynasty. It was also pointed out that the Shuberts (as Bernie and Gerry were commonly known, as if Shubert were an honorific title) had been instrumental in restoring the neighborhood. When they took over

West 45th Street

the Shubert empire in the early '70s, the most sensible step might have been to turn the theaters into parking lots, but Jacobs and Schoenfeld restored all the theaters sumptuously, setting an example for other theater owners.

The **Booth**, of course, is named for an eminent theatrical family (one member of whom unfortunately is better known for an incident in American history than for his theatrical accomplishments.) It too has often hosted one-person shows, like those of Lily Tomlin and Barry Humphries, better known as Dame Edna Everage. It was also the original home of Stephen Sondheim's Pulitzer Prize-winning musical *Sunday in the Park with George*, starring Mandy Patinkin and Bernadette Peters.

Music Box Theater

If any theater can be called beloved, it is the **Music Box**, which was built in 1921 by the producer Sam Harris and the composer Irving Berlin. Originally, it was designed to house revues by Berlin. Harris wanted the theater to be named Irving Berlin's Music Box Theater, but Berlin refused. After Berlin died in 1990, the Shuberts, who co-own the theater, proposed that Berlin's name finally be placed on the marquee, but out of respect for their father's wishes his daughters refused. In its time, the Music Box, which cost $1 million to build, was considered expensive. Nowadays you'd need more than that to produce a single Broadway play. In its intimacy and charm, there is no better-designed theater on Broadway.

Apart from many of Berlin's own shows, the Music Box was home to the first musical to win the Pulitzer Prize, the Gershwins' *Of Thee I Sing*. In 1989 *A Few Good Men*, by a young playwright named Aaron Sorkin, opened here. A year into its successful run, a young actor named Bradley Whitford took over the lead. A few years afterward, playwright and actor teamed together in *The West Wing*.

19

Let's walk east across Broadway. As of this writing there is a restaurant called **Bond 45** on the downtown side of the street—its electric sign mimics the sign of a men's clothing store that stood on Broadway and 44th Street for many decades. In those days Broadway signage also included a waterfall and a Camel sign that blew puffs of smoke over the street.

The **Lyceum**, in the middle of the block, has one of Broadway's most imposing facades, with its grand Roman columns. Its hardwood interior is equally impressive. It opened in 1903, the same year as another masterpiece by the architectural firm of Herts and Tallent, the New Amsterdam. When it opened, it was noted for its inclusion of shops for building sets inside the theater, like the Metropolitan Opera House.

Theaters east of Broadway are often dark, partly because of an old-fashioned way of thinking: if your play was in one of the clusters of theaters on either 44th or 45th Streets you might profit from "walk-in business." The customer wants to buy

Bond 45 restaurant

tickets for X, but they're sold out. Rather than just go home and get to bed early, the customer will rush across the street and buy

tickets for Y. This paradigm for ticket-buying has not been valid for decades, especially since the institution of the TKTS booth in Duffy Square, where last minute theatergoers can get half-price tickets for that day's performances. Nevertheless, the notion that the theaters on this side of Broadway will not get "walk-in business" means they are the last to be rented to producers.

The Lyceum's location may explain why in the early '70s it was home to the APA-Phoenix Theater, which presented classic plays directed by Ellis Rabb, and why, in the late '90s, Tony Randall used it for his Na-

Lyceum Theater

tional Actors Theater. Subscription series do not depend on "walk-in business."

The jumble of little businesses and restaurants that characterized these streets was replaced in the latter decades of the 20th century by the corporate skyscrapers that have made Sixth Avenue the chilling thoroughfare it is, its sidewalks supercrowded during the workday and virtually empty at night. Let's turn back west on 46th Street. The brown stone building on the downtown side of the street, designed in the Romanesque style and finished in 1894, may look familiar—it was the setting for the TV show *Fame*, based on the experiences of kids at the High School of Performing Arts. Among its many famous graduates are Diahann Carroll, Liza Minnelli, and Al Pacino. Along with the High School of Music and Art, Performing Arts was transferred to the Fiorello LaGuardia High School behind Lincoln Center, and this handsome building was reborn as the **Jacqueline Kennedy Onassis High School for International Careers**.

On the northeast corner of 46th Street and Broadway is a reminder of how show business transformed even the most basic commerce. This corner of the **Actors' Equity** building, the headquarters of the actors' union, used to be a branch of the I. Miller shoe store chain. Between the two World Wars a lot of imagination was given to designing shoe stores—though generally the ones on Fifth Avenue. Nowadays shoe stores reflect a more utilitarian mindset. Not many, for example, have stone facades, nor do they have the sort of grand statuary this one does. Look up to the second story and you'll see sculptures of some of its famous clients in their most famous roles: Ethel Barrymore as Ophelia, Marilyn Miller in the title

The Actors' Equity building

21

1

role of Jerome Kern's musical *Sunny,* Mary Pickford as Little Lord Fauntleroy, and—what will come as a surprise to those who forget that grand opera was once part of popular culture—the great soprano Rosa Ponselle in the title role of Bellini's *Norma.* The statues are the work of A. Stirling Calder, who is not as well known as his son, Alexander Calder.

Let's cross onto the island in the middle of the intersection. Technically this triangle is called **Father Duffy Square,** for the man whose statue stands in the middle of the island. Father Duffy was a courageous chaplain during

St. Malachy's Church

World War I who had earlier served as the pastor of **St. Malachy's Church** around the corner west of Broadway on 49th Street, long known as the Actor's Chapel. But first we encounter the statue of a man who was one of the most famous and beloved performers of the first half of the 20th century: George M. Cohan. In his capacity as an actor he had appeared in the original cast of Eugene O'Neill's autobiographical *Ah, Wilderness.* But he was better known as the composer of such songs as "Over There" and "Give My Regards to Broadway."

Since 1973 this island has been best known as the home of the TKTS booth, a project of the Theater Development Fund. It sells half-price and discounted tickets to shows both on and off Broadway a few hours before curtain time. In 1973, not only was this neighborhood itself on the skids, but nearly two-thirds of Broadway theaters were dark. The TKTS booth was intended to stimulate spur-of-the-moment theatergoing.

In those days, when the top price was rarely more than $10, the difference between a half-price theater ticket at $5 and a first-run movie ticket at $2 made the idea of live theater more attractive. The booth became especially popular with out-of-towners, to the extent that a survey of tourists staying in Times Square hotels in

1

the late '90s revealed that they didn't know every theater had its own box office—they thought the way you bought a ticket to a Broadway show was by lining up in Duffy Square.

Let's continue along 46th Street. Two illustrious names face us, **Richard Rodgers** on the left and **Lunt-Fontanne** on the right. Let's start with the Lunt-Fontanne. It was built in 1910 as the Globe by the distinguished producer Charles Dillingham, who unfortunately sustained huge losses in the 1929 stock market crash. He realized that the most profitable way to use the space was to turn it into a movie theater, which it remained until 1958, when it was beautifully renovated and restored to legitimacy with Alfred Lunt and Lynn Fontanne appearing in one of their greatest triumphs, the Swiss playwright Friedrich Duerrenmatt's *The Visit*, directed by Peter Brook.

The Lunts were not just Broadway stars; they were national stars. Throughout their career they toured their shows across the country, performing in theaters of all sizes, sometimes even in high school gymnasiums. Because they were totally dedicated to the craft of acting, they were celebrities without even realizing it. A pair of seats in their theater was dedicated to them. Once, being ushered to their seats for an opening, they heard applause. "There must be someone famous here tonight," Lunt said to his wife. It apparently didn't occur to him that the applause was for them.

Richard Rodgers Theater

1

One of the great titans of New York real estate for much of the 20ᵗʰ century was the Chanin family, best known for an odd, metallic skyscraper across from the Chrysler Building on 42ⁿᵈ Street. In the '20s they built several Broadway theaters, including, in 1924, one that for many years was known by the highly unimaginative name of the 46ᵗʰ Street Theater. In 1990 the producer Alexander

H. Cohen, who had produced Richard Rodgers's last musical, *I Remember Mama*, proposed to the Nederlander Organization that this theater, which they owned, be renamed in Rodgers's honor. It might more fairly have been named the Frank Loesser Theater, since Loesser had two huge hits here, *Guys and Dolls* and *How to Succeed in Business Without Really Trying*. But there are many legendary names that have not received their due—Cole Porter, Tennessee Williams, Arthur Miller, and Jerome Kern, to name just a few.

Paramount Hotel

As we proceed to Eighth Avenue we pass the art deco façade of the **Paramount Hotel**, whose interior underwent a major modernist renovation in the '80s. Its inviting exterior makes a strong contrast to the Marriott Marquis back down the street. Designed in the '70s, when the neighborhood was still very "iffy," the Marquis was built as a fortress to protect its guests from the outside world—even its lobby is on the eighth floor.

Let's walk briskly up Eighth Avenue to 47ᵗʰ Street. Depending on when you read this, you may still be able to look across Eighth to see the hodgepodge of buildings that once constituted this neighborhood, most of which have been replaced by high-rises. As we turn onto 47ᵗʰ Street we see the elegant façade of the **Biltmore**, which was restored in 2003. Its interior is also a gem, an extremely intimate space. It is best known as the home of the musical that caused a sensation in the '60s, *Hair*.

From the late '80s until its acquisition by the Manhattan Theater Club and subsequent restoration, the Biltmore was dark, its interior was vandalized, and it was often reported on the verge of demolition. Its salvation was contingent on a complicated plan that involved building a high-rise around it—this was a case where far-sighted planning benefited the theater. The shortsighted position

1

Biltmore Theater

would have been simply to destroy the theater, which was extremely costly to restore—but enlightened city policy, affording developers tax breaks for preserving the city's history, enabled both economic growth and the retention of an extremely valuable theater.

Across the street from the Biltmore is one of only two Broadway theaters named for critics. The **Brooks Atkinson** honors one of the few *New York Times* critics who might be described as beloved. Atkinson became the critic of the *Times* in 1930 and, except for a hiatus during World War II, when he asked to be assigned to cover the war (and, among other things, reviewed a production of *Hamlet* in China), he remained in that post until 1960.

Brooks Atkinson Theater

1

Ceiling, Café Edison

Ethel Barrymore Theater

A few doors east is the **Edison Hotel**, whose lobby boasts charming art deco murals. It houses a nightclub called **The Supper Club** in a space that was once a theater. Its best known tenant was *Oh, Calcutta!*, which caused a sensation when it opened downtown in 1969 but had lost its shock value when it moved here, providing frissons largely for foreign tourists.

In the '80s its coffee shop, **Café Edison**, was nicknamed the Polish Tea Room. Even the reference that is being parodied now seems a little obscure—the Russian Tea Room, on 57ᵗʰ Street, famously advertised as "slightly to the left of Carnegie Hall," was in its later years a celebrity hangout with an emphasis on Hollywood. When it opened in the '20s, it had indeed been a tearoom whose clientele consisted of White Russians, refugees from the Bolshevik Revolution, many of them involved in the arts. Its décor consisted of antiques from the czarist era.

The Polish Tea Room has no such amenities. It was operated by an elderly couple who were survivors of the Holocaust. In 2001 Neil Simon wrote a play about them titled *45 Seconds from Broadway*. The Polish Tea Room's clientele consisted of people who worked nearby—theater people of the nuts-and-bolts variety, producers, managers, and of course actors.

Across the street is an unusually graceful theater, the **Ethel Barrymore**, which gives the theatergoer a strong sense of proximity to the stage. Unlike the many Broadway theaters that were renamed for stars after they had been standing a long time, this one was named for Barrymore when it was built, in 1928. It has housed many important plays, notably the original 1947 production of Tennessee Williams's *A Streetcar Named Desire*, which catapulted Marlon Brando to stardom, and a revival in 1992 with Alec Baldwin and Jessica Lange.

This time we won't cross Broadway. We'll just look at the **Palace**, which was the destination of vaudeville stars for decades. Many of the office buildings in this neighborhood a century ago were booking offices for theaters across the country. One of the virtues of vaudeville in the eyes of the producers was that the performers provided their own costumes and scenery—all you had to supply was the stage. The Palace has been a Broadway theater for many years—one of its attractions in the late '60s was appropriately a musical about its neighbor George M. Cohan, called *George M.*, with Joel Grey in the title role. The Palace is fondly remembered as a place where Judy Garland gave concerts over the years, including a famous one in 1969 shortly before she died.

Walking up to 48ᵗʰ Street we see the other Broadway theater named for a critic, the **Walter Kerr**. Its renovation was another

1

brainchild of Rocco Landesman. Before its renaming, this theater was called the Ritz, and its interior was fairly mundane. Landesman discovered that the original, more elaborate interior decoration was never completed because funds ran out when the Great Depression took hold. In honor of Kerr, Landesman resurrected the original '20s design, which gave the interior a fairy-tale glow.

Proceeding down 48th Street, we approach the **Longacre**, another nicely proportioned theater suitable for non-musical plays. Here we will call an arbitrary halt to our journey. As we move uptown, more and more of the theaters are surrounded by hotels and high-rises only recently constructed. Besides, this theater serves as a useful bookend, a reminder that the area through which we have walked, a neighborhood with exciting connotations all over the world, was once known largely for its horse trading.

Walter Kerr Theater

WALK TWO

Adolph Green's Daily "Commute"

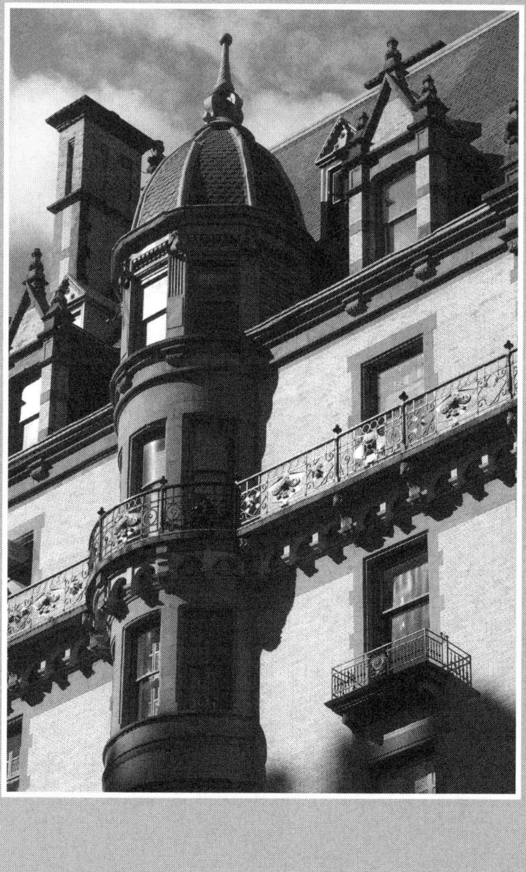

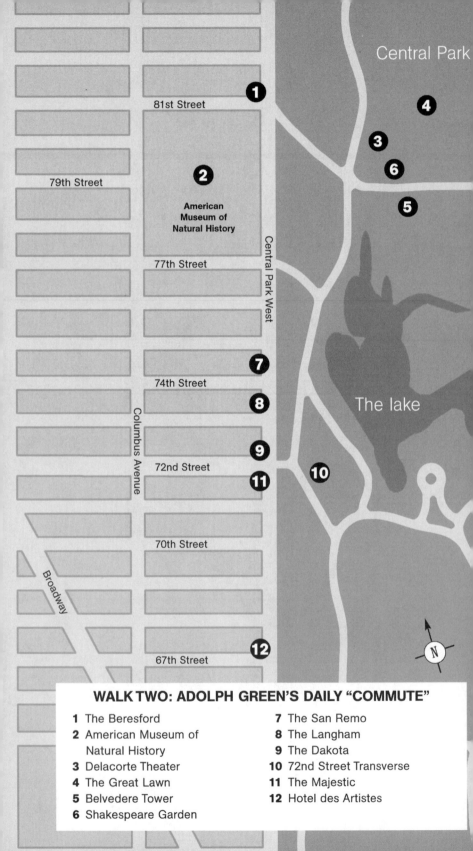

81st Street

Central Park

Central Park West

American Museum of Natural History

79th Street

77th Street

Columbus Avenue

74th Street

72nd Street

Broadway

70th Street

The lake

67th Street

WALK TWO: ADOLPH GREEN'S DAILY "COMMUTE"

1 The Beresford
2 American Museum of
   Natural History
3 Delacorte Theater
4 The Great Lawn
5 Belvedere Tower
6 Shakespeare Garden

7 The San Remo
8 The Langham
9 The Dakota
10 72nd Street Transverse
11 The Majestic
12 Hotel des Artistes

N

Few tributes to New York are as memorable, musically as well as lyrically, as the one that begins, "New York, New York, a helluva town, / The Bronx is up and the Battery's down."

The words came from the first song in *On the Town*, the 1944 musical that introduced Betty Comden, Adolph Green, and Leonard Bernstein to Broadway. (Its choreographer, Jerome Robbins, had already appeared there as a hoofer.)

By the time they wrote those lyrics, Comden and Green had been working together for five years as members of a comedy group called the Revuers, which appeared at a "hot" Greenwich Village club called the Village Vanguard. Their collaboration continued for nearly six decades more. They worked together virtually every day they were both in New York, which was most of the time.

During the '50s Miss Comden lived on East 95th Street, between Lexington and Park, on the same block as Al Hirschfeld. Like most people in the theater, Comden and Green had a special affection for Hirschfeld. They both felt they had truly "arrived" in the theater when, in Boston on the out-of-town tryout for *On the Town*, they learned that Hirschfeld had come up from New York to do a caricature of the show to run in the *New York Times* the Sunday before it opened. This was, of course, years before Betty Comden became his neighbor.

Over the decades, Hirschfeld did many drawings, not just of the shows Comden and Green wrote, but of the two authors themselves. The artist often used visual cues to inspire his drawings. His verbal characterization of Green, he once told a reporter with a chuckle, was "an exploding ventricle."

Our tour begins on the southwest corner of 81st Street and Central Park West. For the last few decades of his life, Green lived in the building across the street from us, the **Beresford**, one of New York's grandest apartment houses. Every day he walked to Comden's apartment on West 67th Street, where she moved a few years before her

The Beresford

death, for their work sessions. Considering that for much of his later life Green was nearly blind, his daily odyssey was, as Comden put it, "courageous." He didn't take the same route every day, but we will take the simplest version of that journey. He did, by the way, go on foot rather than descend the steps into the subway. Although Comden and Green described the subway in their musical *Subways Are for Sleeping* as "that magic train of dreams," they took a more sober view of it in real life.

When the Beresford was finished in 1929, it counted among its architectural distinctions—apart from its three towers—the fact that elevators opened directly into apartments, rather than onto anonymous corridors. Unlike the East Side, from Fifth to slightly east of Park, which was developed to accommodate some of the wealthiest people in the city, if not the world, the West Side, much of which was still farmland until the 1870s, was less socially exclusive.

East Side buildings were openly restrictive (an early 20th-century architectural magazine urged the necessity of "vigilance committees" to ward off "a peroxide Juno . . . or a hook-nosed tenant, of the kind of hook-nose you know and apprehend.") Buildings on the West Side were less carefully policed. The West Side, in fact, was considered a kind of "frontier." In Edith Wharton's 1916 novel *The Custom of the Country*, the family of the quintessential

social climber Undine Spragg, arriving flush with new money from the Middle West, settles on the West Side. Unlike many East Side buildings, which were off limits to theatricals, the West Side welcomed them. When the distinguished actor Edwin Booth bequeathed his Gramercy Park townhouse to The Players, it was to create a place where actors could mingle with "gentlemen" and thus bring down the barriers between them.

Many show business people have lived in the Beresford. A piece of urban mythology—and

American Museum of Natural History

nothing more than that—says that director Mike Nichols once lived in one of the towers facing the park. He is supposed to have had a huge party in which different guests were invited to different towers, and he was the only one able to shuttle between them.

Another of Green's neighbors at the Beresford was Isaac Stern. One of the last times Comden and Green performed in public together was at a memorial tribute to Stern in Carnegie Hall in October 2001. Fellow lyricist Sheldon Harnick and film director Sidney Lumet live here. So do tennis champ John McEnroe and TV comedian Jerry Seinfeld. (Seinfeld also owns a brownstone on a nearby block that he uses to store his vintage autos.) Among previous tenants were the distinguished anthropologist Margaret Meade (since she worked at the museum across the street, it was a quick commute), Hollywood star Rock Hudson, who maintained an apartment here until his death in 1985, and opera diva Beverly Sills until her death in 2007.

Behind us, of course, is the **American Museum of Natural History**, whose dinosaur gallery was the setting for a number in *On the Town* that Comden and Green performed on many occasions, including the tribute to Stern. The song, "Carried Away," is about two people attracted to each other because they are unable, so to speak, to curb their enthusiasms.

We will begin our walk by crossing into Central Park to visit the **Delacorte Theater**, where, in the summer of 1997, a revival of *On the Town* was produced and directed by the then artistic director of the New York Shakespeare Festival, George C. Wolfe. Comden

Delacorte Theater, Central Park

and Green came to the theater almost every night, not just to see how the show was doing but to greet the many friends and fans who attended it. The park also played a featured role in the 1949 film version of *On the Town*. Gene Kelly, Frank Sinatra, and Jules Munshin, as the three sailors on leave, bicycle through the park in the film's opening number.

The Delacorte is named after George Delacorte, the publishing tycoon. It is the lasting legacy of Joseph Papp, who in 1957 started producing free Shakespeare in Central Park. Originally the plays were presented in the open air on the **Great Lawn**, with the atmospheric **Belvedere Tower** in the background. Robert Moses, the powerful parks commissioner, was surprised by how popular they were. In 1962 he insisted Papp charge some admission fee to cover the cost of restoring the grass. Papp refused, and Moses threatened to withdraw permission to continue presenting the plays.

At one point, Papp was on the point of compromise, but his publicist, Merle Debuskey, told him, "I'm willing to work for you for nothing to present free Shakespeare, but I'm not going to do it for cheap Shakespeare." Papp stood his ground and remained one of the few people ever to best Moses.

Even before Papp began presenting Shakespeare here there was a tribute to the world's greatest dramatist in the form of a

Shakespeare Garden, just south of the theater. Every flower and herb in it is mentioned in the plays. The garden also has an oak imported from Stratford-upon-Avon, Shakespeare's hometown.

Returning to Central Park West at 77th Street, we might note that a piece of New York theater that finds a nationwide audience every year, the Macy's Thanksgiving Day Parade, begins in the blocks around the Museum of Natural History, where the huge balloons are inflated. The parade comes down this street, turns onto Broadway, and ends in front of Macy's.

Shakespeare Garden, Central Park

Because New York is a walking city, it has, despite its size, the quality of a small town. On foot you invariably run into people you know. George Lee Andrews, an actor, recalled running into Adolph Green, who was walking down Central Park West with his son Adam one day. Green asked Andrews, who had been in *The Phantom of the Opera* since it opened on Broadway in 1988, what he was doing these days. With a look of resignation, Andrews answered, "As always, Adolph, *Phantom.*"

"Ah, yes," Green exclaimed, looking heavenward and raising his arm as if in a prayerful hosanna and referring to the actor's job security. "Doomed to eternal salvation!"

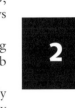

The likelihood of running into friends and colleagues is extremely high on Central Park West. For example, the building we are now passing, the **San Remo**, which runs from 74th to 75th Streets, is or has been home to such movie stars as Dustin Hoffman and Diane Keaton. Green's fellow lyricist Fred Ebb lived here. Raquel Welch sublet an apartment belonging to Barry Manilow when she took over the leading role in the Kander and Ebb musical *Woman of the Year* from Lauren Bacall. The great American ballerina Nora Kaye, who danced in *Fancy Free*, composed by Green's friend Leonard Bernstein, lived in this building with her husband, Herb Ross, the noted choreographer and film director. Another famous resident was the great songwriter Harold Arlen. Current residents include the rock singer Bono, Steven Spielberg, Steve Martin, and the theatrical producers Scott Rudin and James L. Nederlander.

The San Remo

We are now passing 135 Central Park West, the **Langham**, where Lee Strasberg lived for many years. On Sundays the Strasbergs had a "salon" at which you might find such luminaries of the Actor's Studio as Al Pacino, Robert De Niro, Shelley Winters, and Ellen

The Langham

The Dakota

Burstyn. Mia Farrow lives here, as did her onetime lover Woody Allen, who at that time had his own apartment directly across the Park at 75th and Fifth. During their sojourn in Hollywood in the early '50s, Comden and Green worked with Farrow's ex-husband André Previn on the score for the film *It's Always Fair Weather.* Conductor James Levine had an apartment here for many years. Pop singer Carly Simon, who recorded some of Comden and Green's songs on her torch song album, had an apartment here.

We are now across from the **Dakota**, so named because when it was built, in 1870, it was considered as far from civilized New York as the Dakota territory. It was designed by Henry Hardenburgh, who is best known as the designer of the Plaza Hotel and an equally grand building, the Con Edison headquarters, on 14th Street.

Although it has always been a cherished New York landmark, the Dakota became world-famous for two reasons. It was the setting for the enormously successful 1970 film *Rosemary's Baby*, and in 1980 the grandiose entryway was the site of the murder of John Lennon as he was coming home with his wife, Yoko Ono, who still lives here. She subsidized the creation of Strawberry Fields in Central Park in memory of Lennon. Among the famous residents have been Basil Rathbone, Rudolf Nureyev, and, while they were married in the early '50s, José Ferrer and Rosemary Clooney.

Green's closest friend, Leonard Bernstein, lived here. They met in 1937 at a summer camp in the Berkshires called Onota, which was near Pittsfield, Massachusetts. Bernstein, a Boston-born Harvard student, as music counselor was organizing a production of Gilbert and Sullivan's *The Pirates of Penzance*. Green, a Bronx-born high school dropout, came to audition for the Pirate King. After a quick game of one-upmanship in which each managed to stump the other with his knowledge of classical music, they became immediate and lifelong friends.

2

Bernstein and his wife, Felicia, moved to the Dakota in the early '70s, shortly after the cocktail party they threw for the Black Panthers in their Park Avenue apartment, which Tom Wolfe satirized in his book *Radical Chic*. A year before his death in November 1990, Bernstein conducted a complete recording of his masterpiece *Candide* for Deutsche Grammophon starring Green as the optimistic philosopher Pangloss.

Bernstein collaborated with Comden and Green on two classic musicals, *On the Town* and the 1954 *Wonderful Town*, an adaptation of the play *My Sister Eileen*. In the early '60s they began collaborating on a musical version of Thornton Wilder's *The Skin of Our Teeth*. They ran into difficulties and abandoned the project, but Bernstein salvaged one of his tunes and used it to set the 23rd Psalm in his choral piece *Chichester Psalms*.

Another close friend of Green's in the Dakota is Lauren Bacall, who starred in the musical adaptation of *All About Eve* that Comden and Green did with Charles Strouse in 1970. The musical was called *Applause*, and it marked Bacall's musical debut. Comden and Green had the rights to the short story by Mary Orr on which the 1950 Joseph Mankiewicz film was based, but they did not have the rights to his screenplay, which is why many of the celebrated lines from the movie are missing from the show.

Although it would not have been on Green's daily stroll, an adventurous walker might go across the **72nd Street Transverse**, ending up on Fifth Avenue. The modern apartment building on the northeast corner was where Jule Styne lived. Comden and Green first collaborated with him on a revue called *Two on the Aisle* in 1951. A few years later they wrote several songs together for the Mary Martin version of *Peter Pan*, including the iconic "Never Never Land." In 1956 they created *Bells Are Ringing* as a vehicle for their fellow Revuer Judy Holliday, who also lived in the Dakota.

It was in the chorus of *Bells Are Ringing* that Green met his wife, Phyllis Newman. In a subsequent collaboration with Styne, *Subways Are for Sleeping*, Newman played a former Southern beauty queen. Her showstopping song, "Shoo-in," won her a Tony in the spring of 1962, beating a newcomer by the name of Barbra Streisand.

Among the other shows Comden and Green wrote with Styne were the 1960 *Do Re Mi*, which starred Phil Silvers and Nancy Walker, and the 1962 *Fade Out Fade In*, which showcased the talents of Carol Burnett.

Continuing down Central Park West, we are passing the **Majestic** on the southwest corner of 72nd Street, which is where Burton Lane, the composer of *Finian's Rainbow* and *On a Clear Day You Can See Forever*, used to live. So did the quintessential gossip columnist Walter Winchell and the brilliant Broadway and Hollywood director Elia Kazan. The first work by Comden and Green ever to be recorded was one of their Village Vanguard sketches, "The Girl with Two Left Feet," a satire of Hollywood that includes a gossip columnist called Winter Walchell.

Needless to say, not all the people who live in these buildings are in show business. A longtime tenant was underworld czar Frank Costello, who survived an assassination attempt in the building lobby. On another note, an interesting bit of trivia about the Majestic is that one of the men who worked on it as a carpenter when it was built in 1931 was Bruno Richard Hauptman, who was later convicted of kidnapping the Lindbergh baby.

We will turn west at 67th Street, which is quite unlike any side street on the West Side. Most West Side streets are filled with brownstones, which a century ago were single-family dwellings. Over the years, especially during the Depression, they could no longer be sustained by single families and were broken down into smaller apartments or, in some cases, single-room occupancy hotels.

But 67th Street started out as tall apartment buildings with very specific tenants in mind. The buildings offered studios and living spaces for artists—not the beginners who lived in cramped Bohemian quarters in the Village, but successful artists who were expected to display their work in grand salons for their equally grand patrons.

Several of the buildings on this block consist of duplex apartments in the front and conventional one-story apartments in back. The two-story spaces enabled painters to work on huge canvases—life-size portraits, for example, which were the lifeblood of society painters. The eminent illustrator Leroy Nieman and the film director Arthur Penn live on this block, as did the distinguished photographer Arnold Newman.

At the turn of the 20th century, artists and illustrators were often celebrities of the magnitude of today's movie stars. That was certainly the case with Howard Chandler Christy, who resided in the **Hotel des Artistes** on the corner. In the '30s he was invited to paint the slightly naughty murals of nude wood nymphs that have decorated the walls of the Café des Artistes on the ground floor ever since. Among the other luminaries who have lived in the Hotel des Artistes are former Mayor John Lindsay, Isadora Duncan, Noel Coward, and perhaps the last of the celebrity illustrators, Norman Rockwell.

During the early '40s one of the block's residents was Bernstein. As Green walked down this street he may have remembered the many days and nights he and Betty and Lenny sat around Bernstein's piano writing *On the Town*.

On the sliver of a 67th Street between Columbus and Broadway, there used to be a sliver of a bookstore called Applause, which later moved to a larger store on 71st Street and blossomed into the

Hotel des Artistes

theatrical and film publishing house. If you had squeezed into the store in its original, cramped location, you might have been waited on by a Juilliard student named Bradley Whitford.

We are now approaching Broadway, which is full of high-rise apartments that can only be rented by young stockbrokers and financial analysts. This is a far cry from Waverly Place, where the actors and painters and writers of *Wonderful Town* came to conquer New York. Each high-rise represents the destruction of at least a few dozen brownstones that might have been home to a young Betty or Adolph.

Until Thanksgiving of 2006 when she died, Betty lived in the high-rise at the corner of 67th and Amsterdam, with windows that looked downtown toward a quintessential view of "New York, New York."

WALK THREE

A Walk
Through the Life
of Irving Berlin

WALK THREE: A WALK THROUGH THE LIFE OF IRVING BERLIN

1 112 West 38th Street
2 New Amsterdam Theater
3 224 West 44th Street
4 St. James Theater
5 Shubert Alley
6 Booth Theater
7 Music Box Theater
8 Imperial Theater

9 Broadway Theater
10 Warwick Hotel
11 Radio City Music Hall
12 29 West 46th Street
13 Omni Berkshire Place
14 The Waldorf-Astoria Hotel
15 17 Beekman Place

Anyone who knows anything about Irving Berlin would as-sume that a walking tour based on his life would have to start on the Lower East Side. But you could actually say Berlin was born at **112 West 38th Street**. A few explanatory words are called for. Someone named Israel Baline was born in the town of Temun in Siberia in 1888. At the age of five, escaping hardship and pogroms, he and his family fled to America and took up resi-dence in a tenement on Cherry Street. His father, who had been a cantor in the old country, became a kosher butcher, and as soon as he was able, little Izzy was on the streets helping the family earn a living. As a teenager he worked as a singing waiter in some of the many restaurants on the Lower East Side.

In 1907, "Marie from Sunny Italy," with lyrics by young Israel, was published by the firm of Joseph W. Stern & Co., which had of-fices in this building. It was Baline's first published song. The type-setter, unable to read the lyricist's handwriting, transcribed the last name as Berlin and left the first as the initial I. The lyricist liked it. For his first name he chose Irving, one of those WASP names fre-quently chosen by Jewish immigrants who wanted to sound more "American." Little did he know how deep an impact he would have on what sounded American.

As we walk toward Broadway we should keep in mind that 100 years ago these streets were filled with much smaller buildings than the ones that stand here now, with a huge variety of businesses on their ground floors—in many cases, restaurants with live mu-sic.

This neighborhood, which we think of as the garment cen-ter, was not yet associated with any one business, unless it was show business. If, here at the corner of Broadway and 38th, you looked downtown, you saw the lights of theater after the-ater—far more, in 1909, than if you looked uptown. Tin Pan Alley, the heart of the pop mu-sic business, was centered down on 28th Street, but its tentacles

Berlin's figurative birthplace

43

reached all through this area, including the firm that, so to speak, "baptized" Irving Berlin. Early in his career, when Berlin began to publish his own music, he had his office in the building where he was "named."

As we begin our walk through Irving Berlin's life, we will pass through the neighborhood where he earned his living. Show business has always been an integral part of New York's economy, and at the beginning of the 20th century it dominated this area.

On the southeast corner of Broadway and 39th Street stood the Moorish turreted Casino Theater, which had been home to some of Gilbert and Sullivan's greatest American successes. At the turn of the century it housed a British musical blockbuster called *Floradora*, which was famous for its sextet of beauties singing the hit song, "Tell Me, Pretty Maiden, Are There Any More at Home Like You?" All six of the original Floradora girls married millionaires. In fact, because the Florodora beauties were constantly finding wealthy husbands or protectors, the turnover was so great that in its first smash year 73 girls played these coveted roles.

On the northwest corner of Broadway and 39th you had another sort of show business, called the Metropolitan Opera House. It

occupied the entire block between 39th and 40th, between Broadway and Seventh. In the late 19th and early 20th centuries, opera was a form of popular entertainment. If there had been a hit parade back then, it would have been filled with opera arias, which would have been familiar to every part of the city's population. You would have heard them as often as the popular hits of the day in the many cafés in the neighborhood that catered to the 3,000 people a night who attended the Metropolitan.

Broadway and 38th Street, looking south

In one such café, André Bustanoby's Bistro across from the Met, the band was conducted by its pianist, Sigmund Romberg, who had been born in Hungary in 1887, a year before Berlin's birth in Russia. Romberg, who had a degree in engineering, emigrated here in 1909. Unlike Berlin, whose music came from the streets of New York with an undercurrent of melancholy that perhaps reflected his ethnic heritage, Romberg's music sounds more like the operettas of the Austro-Hungarian Empire. In the Bustanoby Bistro, Romberg played his own compositions alongside better-known music. It was here that he was discovered by Florenz Ziegfeld, who commissioned him to write numbers for his revues in the new theaters further up Broadway.

It was Ziegfeld who also brought Irving Berlin into the theater, interpolating some of his songs into the 1910 and 1911 editions of the Ziegfeld Follies. The first show for which Berlin provided the entire score was "Watch Your Step," which starred the renowned dancing team of Vernon and Irene Castle. It opened December 8, 1914, here at the **New Amsterdam Theater**, which we will find just west of Seventh Avenue on 42nd Street.

The New Amsterdam was where many of the Ziegfeld Follies were presented. Among the songs Berlin contributed to these shows over several decades were "A Pretty Girl Is Like a Melody," "Shaking the Blues Away," and "Mandy."

Not all the shows that played here were froth. In 1933, Berlin and playwright Moss Hart wrote a revue called *As Thousands Cheer*, each of whose songs was based on some contemporary event indicated by a newspaper headline. Among those songs were "Heat Wave" and "Easter Parade." Much of the show was satiric, but at one point the stage was filled with the front page of a tabloid that blared, "UNKNOWN NEGRO LYNCHED BY FRENZIED MOB." The curtain rose on Ethel Waters setting the dinner table and singing to her children, knowing full well that their father would not be coming home. The song was "Supper Time," one of Berlin's most powerful creations. Waters herself said, "If one song can tell the whole tragic history of a race, 'Supper Time' was that song."

Roof gardens were popular at the turn of the century—covered so they could provide entertainment all summer long, even if it rained. They were the forerunner of what would eventually become nightclubs. The New Amsterdam Roof was one of the most popular of these nightspots. There are plans to restore it.

Throughout the teens, when Berlin was writing hit after hit, his songs were heard in the theaters and cabarets that lined these streets. Sometimes our walk has to make allowances for chronol-

3

ogy. We're going to make our way up Seventh Avenue and turn left on 44th Street to stop at **number 224**, which during World War II became the Stage Door Canteen, immortalized in Berlin's "I Lost My Heart at the Stage Door Canteen."

The canteen was in the basement of what had been a former speakeasy known as the Little Club. The Shuberts, who owned the building, donated the space. It opened on March 4, 1942, barely three months after America entered World War II. Subsequently, canteens opened in Washington, Philadelphia, Boston, Cleveland, Trenton, Newark, San Francisco, and Hollywood, as well as London and Paris.

The manager of the Times Square Canteen was Kermit Bloomgarden, an accountant who would later go on to become the producer of such American classics as Arthur Miller's *Death of a Salesman*, Meredith Willson's *The Music Man*, and Stephen Sondheim's short-lived but legendary *Anyone Can Whistle*. Food and soft drinks were donated by restaurants, dance music by famous bands.

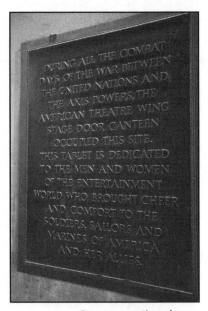

Commemorative plaque, the Stage Door Canteen

From 6 P.M. to midnight, lines a block long waited to get in. An average of 3,000 soldiers per night came through. They were entertained by such figures as the actor Alfred Lunt, the writer Carl Van Vechten, and actresses Shirley Booth, Celeste Holm, Gypsy Rose Lee, and her sister, June Havoc. The Canteen was sponsored by the Wing, which is now best known as the sponsor of the Tonys. The Wing was short for American Theater Wing of British War Relief, which was started in 1939, just after the Nazis invaded Poland. The Canteen was only one of the war services of all kinds that the Wing provided. One of the most active supporters of the Canteen was the actress Antoinette Perry, nicknamed Tony, for whom the Tony Awards were named when they began in 1947.

As we look down 44th Street we see the **St. James Theater**, which housed Irving Berlin's last Broadway show, *Mr. President*, starring Robert Ryan and Nanette Fabray. It opened in the fall of 1962, when Berlin was already 74, and despite lukewarm reviews managed an eight-month run. It had two memorable songs, both of which reflected its old-fashioned flavor. One was "Let's Go Back to the Waltz." The other was "This Is a Great Country," one of Berlin's finest patriotic songs, written at a time when patriotism itself was beginning to seem outdated.

We're going to cross the street now and walk through **Shubert Alley**, so named because the Shuberts, once the most powerful of theater owners and producers, had their headquarters above the theater that bears their

St. James Theater

name. Subsequent heads of the organization, whatever their names, are still referred to as the Shuberts. The original Shuberts built and owned half the theaters in this neighborhood, including the **Booth**, which is at the other end of "their" alley. Until the late '60s the other "wall" of Shubert Alley was the back of the Astor Hotel, which was demolished in 1968 to construct the undistinguished skyscraper that now stands here.

Looking across 45th Street, we see the **Music Box Theater**. It opened in 1921 with the first Music Box Revue, which con-

tained one of Berlin's most infectious songs, "Say It with Music." The revues were produced annually during the early '20s and contained such other Berlin perennials as "What'll I Do?," "Who," and "Three Cheers for the Red, White and Blue."

The theater next door, the **Imperial**, is quite a large house, but like the Music Box it is beautifully proportioned, and over the years it housed some of Berlin's biggest hits,

Shubert Alley

47

starting with his underrated 1940 *Louisiana Purchase*. The Music Box Revues of the '20s provided many of Berlin's best known songs, but the shows themselves would be hard to revive because the humor of the sketches has dated considerably. The same is true of *Miss Liberty*, the 1948 show at the Imperial that Berlin wrote with the Pulitzer Prize—winning playwright Robert Sherwood. This fanciful, completely fictional account of how the Statue of Liberty was created is best remembered for the perennial favorite "Let's Take an Old Fashioned Walk," and for Berlin's haunting choral setting of Emma Lazarus's poem "The New Colossus," which is inscribed on the statue's pedestal.

The other two Berlin musicals that played here require no introduction. One was the 1946 *Annie Get Your Gun*, which starred Ethel Merman and whose score contains such favorites as "They Say That Falling in Love Is Wonderful," "The Girl That I Marry," "I've Got the Sun in the Morning and the Moon at Night," and "Anything You Can Do." (When it was revived at Lincoln Center in 1966, again starring Merman, Berlin wrote a new song for her, "An Old-Fashioned Wedding," his last composition for the theater.)

In 1951 Merman and Berlin scored another triumph at the Imperial with *Call Me Madam*, based roughly on the career of Perle Mesta, the Washington social hostess turned ambassadress. The action takes place in the mythical European country of Lichtenberg, obviously modeled on the tiny country of Lichtenstein, which will

play a role later in our walk. It was in *Call Me Madam* that Russell Nype sang, "I smell blossoms but the trees are bare," and Merman told him, "You're not sick/ You're just in love."

Despite his international fame, Berlin led an oddly circumscribed life. During most of his career, he lived only a few blocks away from these theaters. (Even in his final years, when his lodgings were grander, he was not too far from where he had made his living.) He also had his office and the office of

Broadway and 51st Street, the site of one of Berlin's offices

his music publishing businesses in the middle of the theater district. As we have noted, his first publishing firm was in the building where we began our tour. Later it moved to 799 Broadway, closer to Tin Pan Alley.

For many decades, the firm was located a block down from the Brill Building, at 52nd Street, which was the headquarters for Tin Pan Alley in its latter days. Berlin always wanted to keep his firm separate from the others. His own office was on the second floor of the building on the southeast corner of 51st Street and Broadway, which is now the showroom for Capezio, the dancewear manufacturer. The showroom, which is open to the public during normal business hours, has several display cases of shows worn—and autographed—by famous hoofers, from Broadway greats Gwen Verdon and Liza Minnelli to Mikhail Baryshnikov.

Let's walk up to the **Broadway Theater**, which stands between 52nd and 53rd Streets. It was here, on an evening in 1942, that Berlin enjoyed one of his greatest triumphs. By the time that World War II began he was a little old to fight, but he wanted to be involved. In what better way could he have given his services than

3

by writing a show, as he had done during the First World War? That one was titled *Yip! Yip! Yaphank*. This one was called *This Is the Army*, and it contained the song "This Is the Army, Mr. Jones." It also contained a song Berlin had written for his earlier show, "Oh, How I Hate to Get Up in the Morning."

The opening night for *This Is the Army* was, fittingly enough, July 4, 1942. It was an unusually glittering evening, a benefit for the Army Emergency Relief Fund. Kate Smith, for example, paid $10,000 for her two tickets. She was famous for singing a song that had been dropped from *Yip! Yip! Yaphank* but had been dusted off as clouds of war began to materialize in 1939: "God Bless

Broadway Theater

49

3

Broadway Theater

America." (The royalties for this song, by the way, which have been millions over the years, have always gone to the Boy Scouts.)

In the middle of the second act of *This Is the Army*, the curtain rose on a lone figure waking up on an army cot. It was Berlin himself. For the first act he had been seated in a box, watching the show. But at the beginning of the second act he slipped backstage and changed his tuxedo for an enlisted man's uniform. From the introductory chords the audience knew the song they were going to hear was "Oh, How I Hate to Get Up in the Morning." But when they recognized who was going to sing it they stood and applauded for a full ten minutes before letting him sing.

In his review the next morning, John Chapman of the *Daily News* correctly surmised that although Berlin's voice was, as he put it, "squealy and husky," that night "he would have drawn audiences away had Caruso been singing across the street."

The show remained at the Broadway Theater for many months, where free seats were always put aside for soldiers in uniform, but versions were performed all over the world, raising huge sums for the war effort.

Let's walk up a block to 54th Street and start going east. Here at the corner of 54th and Sixth Avenue is the **Warwick Hotel**, which is best known as the place where the Beatles stayed on their first visit to America in 1964, but the Berlin family stayed here in 1932 while their triplex penthouse at 86th Street and East End Avenue was being readied. We'll walk downtown on the east side of Sixth Avenue.

Starting in the '30s, Berlin began to spend a lot of time in Hollywood. Many of the scores for the films with which he was involved were simply compilations of his already-famous hits. "Easter Parade," for example, which was a reworking of an unsuccessful song he had written many years earlier called "Smile and Show Your Dimple," appeared in the 1938 movie *Alexander's Ragtime Band* as well as the 1948 *Easter Parade*.

An exception to this anthology approach was the 1936 film *Follow the Fleet*, which starred Fred Astaire, Ginger Rogers, and, in a small part, Lucille Ball. It was an entirely original score that contained such gems as "Let Yourself Go," "I'd Rather Lead a Band," and "Let's Face the Music and Dance." It opened at **Radio City Music Hall**, which we're now passing. The Music Hall is such a beloved institution that it's hard to imagine that in the late '70s, when New York was still a financially beleaguered city, plans were afoot to convert it into office space like the rest of Rockefeller Center.

3

We'll walk down Sixth Avenue to 46th Street, turn left, and stop in front of **number 29**. In 1921, Berlin bought this building. He was already a phenomenally wealthy man, a celebrity, but it is interesting to see that he did not choose to flaunt his success. He could

Warwick Hotel **Radio City Music Hall**

29 West 46th Street

easily have bought a townhouse or a grand apartment farther uptown. Instead, he bought this six-story building in the middle of what was still a largely residential block with many small businesses at the ground level. On the first floor of his building, in fact, was a grocery store, like the tenement where he had grown up on Cherry Street. On the next three floors were various tenants.

Berlin himself occupied the top two floors. The one concession he made to his success was that he installed an elevator to take him up. At this point he was a widower and a bachelor and had several servants to attend to his needs. But, like generations of hardworking men before him, he combined where he lived with where he worked.

Because he was so close to the theater district, he could easily invite people over. Sometimes people would drop in on him because they knew that, more often than not, they would find him working. Many years afterward, Helen Hayes recalled that during her long courtship with Charles MacArthur, best remembered as the coauthor of *The Front Page*, while they waited for MacArthur's angry wife to consent to a divorce, they often dropped in on Berlin on the way home from whatever theater she was playing.

One night, she recalled, Berlin had just finished a song, and he wanted them to hear it. She and MacArthur listened as he sat at the piano and sang them "Always," which thereafter they considered "their" song. A few years later, Berlin thought it would work in a show he wrote for the Marx Brothers called *The Cocoanuts,* but when he played it for the director, George S. Kaufman, Kaufman sneered that the opening line, "I'll be loving you—always," was unrealistic. He suggested Berlin change it to "I'll be loving you—Thursday." Berlin withdrew the song.

We'll continue walking east until we reach Madison Avenue, where we'll turn uptown. At 50th Street we'll stop and glance a few blocks up to the corner of 52nd Street, where stands the **Omni Berkshire Place** hotel, for many years the home of Ethel Merman. In addition to the two Broadway triumphs she enjoyed with Berlin, Merman appeared in his last full-fledged Hollywood musical, the 1954 *There's No Business Like Show Business.* At the memorial trib-

Omni Berkshire Place

ute to Berlin, Sam Goldwyn, the son of Hollywood mogul Samuel Goldwyn, recalled that as a little boy he had met Berlin and had no idea what he did. Berlin's daughter Mary Ellin, the young Goldwyn's school chum, explained to him that her father wrote songs "for a Miss Merman and sometimes the way she sings them makes him very angry."

Now we'll walk east on 50th Street toward Park Avenue. As we approach Park we see the grand **Waldorf-Astoria Hotel**. On 50th Street there is a tower with a separate entrance. This part of the hotel has a presidential suite, which is where most presidents stay when they come to New York. More important for our purposes, the Waldorf Towers was for many years the home of Berlin's good friend Cole Porter.

It's hard to imagine two men who came from such different worlds as did Berlin and Porter. Porter was born into great wealth in Peru, Indiana, and was educated at Yale when it was at its most snobbish. He then married even greater wealth and spent the '20s living frivolously in Paris. Berlin, as we know, was born into the direst poverty and spent his childhood in the poorest quarter of this city. And yet the two became devoted friends. At a time when Porter despaired of ever getting a show on Broadway, Berlin, already well estab-

The Waldorf-Astoria Hotel

3

lished, gave him the encouragement and help he needed. Over the years they formed a mutual admiration society.

Let's walk through the lobby of the Waldorf, which takes us from Park to Lexington. It is a splendid example of the art deco style that was synonymous with chic in the '20s and early '30s. This hotel replaced another of the same name that once stood at the corner of Fifth Avenue and 34th Street but was torn down to make way for the Empire State Building. The beautiful clock that stands in the center of the lobby was taken from the old Waldorf.

The piano in Peacock Alley, just across from the clock, is Porter's piano. Among the features of this very elegant hotel is a ballroom that is three stories high. Often the party after the Tony Awards takes place here.

Also, and this might be useful the next time you visit New York, below the hotel is a seldom-used platform for a track. If you happen to have a private railroad car, a switching engine can bring it up the street from Grand Central Terminal and save you the hassle of finding a taxi—though it's probably not good form to arrive at the Waldorf from the basement. The servants can take care of transporting the luggage upstairs.

We'll walk East on 49th Street until we reach **Beekman Place**. At number 17 is the townhouse where Berlin spent the last few de-

17 Beekman Place

cades of his life. Fittingly, after he died, the building was bought by the government of Lichtenstein, the model for the duchy of Lichtenberg in *Call Me Madam*.

For most of the 20th century Beekman Place was synonymous with fashion, beyond the wildest dreams of a little boy growing up on the Lower East Side. When people pointed out the disparity between where he had begun and where he had wound up, Berlin was fond of saying that the sounds were the same—the foghorns, the choppy splashes of the waves as tugboats pulled their charges along the river. He was now just a few miles uptown.

WALK FOUR

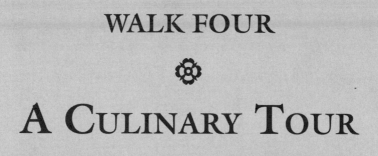

A CULINARY TOUR

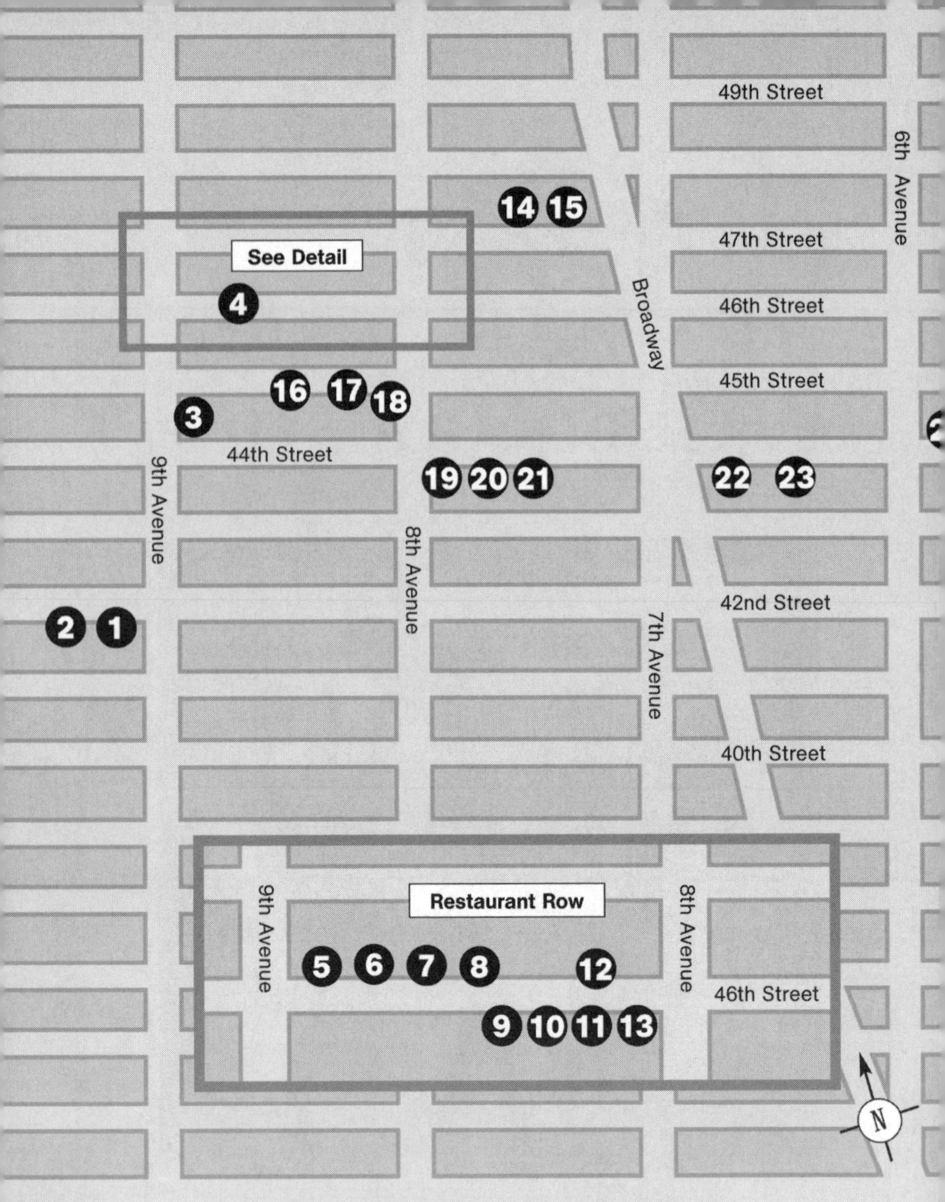

49th Street

6th Avenue

14 15

See Detail

Broadway

47th Street

4

46th Street

45th Street

16 17 18

3

44th Street

19 20 21

22 23

8th Avenue

7th Avenue

42nd Street

2 1

9th Avenue

40th Street

Restaurant Row

9th Avenue

5 6 7 8

12

9 10 11 13

8th Avenue

46th Street

N

WALK FOUR: A CULINARY TOUR

1 Chez Josephine
2 Playwrights Horizons
3 Jezebel
4 Restaurant Row
5 Hourglass Tavern
6 Lattanzi
7 Becco
8 Don't Tell Mama
9 Joe Allen's
10 Orso
11 Bar Centrale
12 Barbetta

13 B. Smith's
14 Café Edison
15 Edison Hotel
16 Sam's
17 Barrymore's
18 Frankie and Johnnie's
19 Angus McIndoe
20 Sardi's
21 Carmine's
22 Virgil's Real Barbecue
23 Osteria al Doge
24 The Algonquin Hotel

I t's been some years since restaurants replaced theater as the prime topic of New York dinner conversation, but even before that happened, restaurants in the theater district played a vital role in the life of the theater. Today they hold an enormous amount of theater history within their walls.

We're going to start with a relative newcomer, **Chez Josephine**, which has been on this site, 420 West 42nd Street, since 1986. What is interesting is that, less than ten years before that, no restaurant of any quality would have wanted to be on this block, let alone on either side of it. Starting in the mid-'60s, 42nd Street from Seventh Avenue to the Hudson was one of the city's great disaster areas— block upon block of shady movie houses, massage parlors, and porn video stores, not to mention bars and strip joints.

In the late '70s an effort was made to turn around what seemed an irreversible trend by acquiring the property on this block and turning what were then decaying brownstones over to Off-Off-

Chez Josephine

Playwrights Horizons

Broadway theater groups. The most successful of them was **Play-wrights Horizons**, which began its life in the early '70s in the YWCA a few blocks up the equally unsavory Eighth Avenue. Playwrights Horizons was to become the home of such Pulitzer Prize–winning works as Stephen Sondheim's *Sunday in the Park with George* and Wendy Wasserstein's *The Heidi Chronicles,* both of which moved to Broadway after successful runs at the modest predecessor of this rather grand-looking theater.

At one point the chairman of the board of Playwrights Horizons was Mary Rubin, the wife of Robert Rubin, Secretary of the Treasury under President Clinton. For a long time both Rubins were fixtures at Chez Josephine. Mary was able to raise the money to build this new theater, which was not exactly what the real estate forces that had originally sponsored Theater Row had hoped for. They wanted theaters to make the neighborhood respectable, to revive the surrounding real estate and make possible new ventures, but had not counted on any of the theaters being solvent enough to bifurcate the block and prevent a block-long development. On the other side of Dyer Avenue there will indeed be a block-wide structure developed by the same firm that created the Time-Warner complex on Columbus Circle. At one time, huge buildings included theaters because this enabled them to add extra floors that would contribute huge revenues. Now the amounts of money available no longer require such sops to the arts.

On the site of a massage parlor and a short-lived French restaurant, Jean-Claude Baker, the adoptive son of Josephine Baker, the African-American dancer, actress, and singer who captivated Paris for five decades, built this tribute to his mother. The walls are covered with murals depicting the glamorous Josephine at her most bewitching. There is also a mural of Chez Josephine's celebrity clientele. Jean-Claude, like Josephine, has always been appreciative of young talent. At one point he hired a kid from New Orleans to play the piano. The kid has done very well. His name is Harry Connick, Jr.

Let's walk east toward Ninth Avenue, which for many years retained an old-fashioned flavor as a street of ethnic grocery stores and open-air markets. As you can see, in recent years it has been gentrified and is now home to many restaurants. At the corner of

45th Street, **Jezebel** has been serving high-priced soul food for decades.

Just as 42nd Street between Ninth and Tenth Avenues was known as Theater Row, we're making our way to 46th Street between Eighth and Ninth, which is still known as **Restaurant Row.** The street's proximity to so many Broadway theaters probably made the proliferation of restaurants inevitable. The range of cuisines and prices is quite extraordinary.

4

Jezebel

Restaurant Row

Hourglass Tavern

4

Lattanzi

Two of the most reasonable restaurants in this neighborhood are close to the western end of the block: the **Hourglass Tavern** and its tasty, reasonable Chilean neighbor **Pomaire**. The Hourglass, which must also be one of the oldest restaurants in this neighborhood, has an hourglass above each of its tables. If business is good, the hourglass will be turned and you will be guaranteed a three-course meal in exactly an hour, at which time you must surrender your table to people waiting in line.

Next come two notable Italian restaurants, **Lattanzi** and **Becco**. Lattanzi specializes in the cuisine developed by Roman Jews. Jews

4

Becco

Don't Tell Mama   Joe Allen's

have been a part of the Eternal City since ancient times. The reasonably priced Becco is the theater district branch of the Bastianich family, which owns some of New York's most illustrious (and expensive) restaurants, such as Felidia and Babbo.

Down the street is **Don't Tell Mama**, one of the city's most enterprising cabarets and a place where many young performers get their start. One of the landmarks of Restaurant Row is **Joe Allen's**, on the south side of the street. Over three decades old, Joe Allen's has always been a moderately priced restaurant that

serves as a hangout for performers. Like many restaurants all over the city, it has bare brick walls as its decorative motif, but what sets it apart is that those walls are covered with posters of some of Broadway's most famous flops, including such one-night stands as *Rockabye Hamlet*—you guessed it, a rock version of Shakespeare's play—and the legendary *Moose Murders*, which *New York Times* theater critic Frank Rich called "a watershed for connoisseurs of disasters."

Orso

62

With the income from Joe Allen, Mr. Allen created **Orso**, right next door. Orso is higher-priced, culinarily more ambitious, and one of the theater district's best places for spotting "names." It seems to be one of the few places in this neighborhood where Hollywood celebrities feel comfortable dining before or after seeing their friends in Broadway shows.

Between the two restaurants you will notice 12 steps leading up to a rather grand set of doors. Until early in 2007 a discreet sign hung above the doors, reading "Bar Centrale."

Barbetta

The sign was removed because by then the only people who mattered already knew it was Bar Centrale, and this tiny little place with a limited but excellent menu was not intended for hoi polloi. Matthew Broderick is often seen here. So are Nathan Lane, Harvey Fierstein, and many other Broadway celebs.

One of the most venerable restaurants on the block is **Barbetta**, across the street. Where most Italian restaurants in this neighborhood were mom-and-pop operations dispensing fare on the order of spaghetti and meatballs, Barbetta served northern Italian cuisine well before it was common in New York. Its interior also has an elegance not common to this neighborhood. On the south side of 46th Street just before we reach Eighth Avenue is **B. Smith's**, the restaurant of former model and lifestyle guru Barbara Smith.

Let's turn left on Eighth and go up to 47th Street. The major culinary landmark on this block is the down-to-earth **Café Edison**. This is one of those places where a person may have eaten without knowing what it was. It's the coffee shop in the Edison Hotel in the middle of the block, and is known as the Polish Tea Room. The title is an ironic reference to the legendary Russian Tea Room on 57th Street, at one time probably the city's most famous celebrity hangout. Its stars were drawn from stage and screen, from the literary world, and of course from the world of classical music.

By contrast, the Polish Tea Room was strictly a theater hangout. And where the Russian Tea Room charges high prices, the Polish Tea Room, run by two immigrants from Eastern Europe, charges

4

Café Edison

next to nothing for its Old World soups and blintzes. The closest it comes to "exclusivity" is a little roped-off area reserved for the heads of the three companies that own all the theaters in the neighborhood: the Shuberts, the Jujamcyns, and the Nederlanders. The sense of irony at the Polish Tea Room is as thick as the aroma of borscht.

Let's cut through the lobby of the Edison, with its simple art deco design, to 46th Street, look left to the northwest corner at Broadway, and observe a moment of silence for a landmark that stood in Times Square for many decades and closed abruptly in the summer of 2005: Howard Johnson's.

Visitors from other cities may be well acquainted with Howard Johnson's, a national chain that once had two branches in the theater district. Even New Yorkers may not realize how remarkable this once was. Until the '70s New York had its own chains of restaurants—the Automat, of which there were several in this neighborhood, Chock full o'Nuts, Riker's (with its slogan employing the Big Lie technique, "No Better Food at Any Price"), and Bickford's. But the only national chain with a presence in this city was Howard Johnson's. Another local landmark long gone was Hector's, which had two faucets—one for what was then the world's most delicious beverage, New York City tap water, and another for seltzer.

Everything changed in 1971 when the first McDonald's opened in Manhattan on the Upper West Side. (Lest you imagine New Yorkers are all that jaded or sophisticated, it's worth remembering that at that late date, when the rest of the country had been acquainted with the Whopper for many years, a line formed around the block so people could be among the first to sample these culinary wonders in New York.)

It was altogether fitting that Howard Johnson's flourished for so long in Times Square, for it owed its early success to the theater. Howard Johnson's was a young, ambitious restaurant in Quincy, a suburb of Boston, in 1928 when the mayor of Boston, without having read the play, banned Eugene O'Neill's *Strange Interlude* from being performed there on its pre-Broadway tour. Fortunately, there was a well-equipped theater nearby in Quincy. So the play, which starred Lynn Fontanne, booked that theater and attracted a very sophisticated audience to the suburban town. O'Neill wrote his play in nine acts, and his first concept was to play it in two separate evenings. Then its director suggested that it might be more effective to play it in one evening with a dinner interlude between acts five and six. The only place to eat near the theater was Howard Johnson's, which made a fortune during the brief run of the play.

When we began this tour on 42nd Street, we recalled the '70s, when the neighborhood was in ruins. An even sadder instance of how destitute New York was in those years is the fact that in the late '70s an Atlanta real estate developer named Portman was able to buy much of the block between 45th and 46th Streets to put up the hotel that stands before us, the **Marriott Marquis**. Its banal design reflects the mentality of an out-of-towner who imagined

4

Passageway, the Marriott Marquis Hotel

that New York was a fearful place and placed the lobby of the hotel on the eighth floor, as if proximity to the street could only invite danger. The hotel has a theater with decent proportions albeit an interior design every bit as banal as the rest of the building. That eighth-floor lobby, by the way, is in the center of the building and has elevators in glass shafts running up to the residential floors. The effect is that of a maximum-security prison.

To erect it, three grand old theaters had to be destroyed. One was the tiny Bijou, known during its latter days as the longtime home of a wordless piece of theater called *Mummenschanz*. One was named for Helen Hayes. When it was demolished, a smaller theater on 44th Street (named, appropriately enough, the Little Theater) was renamed for her. Theatergoers of a certain age will remember a bitter March day in 1982 when one wall of the Morosco had fallen to the wrecking ball and one could look in and see rows of red curtains waiting, dignity intact, for the end. It was a sign of how benighted New York had become that the destruction of theaters with great histories and the erection of this soulless place were regarded as Progress.

The one amenity the Marquis provides is a passageway from 46th Street to 45th, which is the most vibrant block in the theater district, both because of the number of theaters and the number of restaurants.

The theaters along this street are considered particularly desirable because of producers' belief in "walk-in business." They imagine that theatergoers, unable to get tickets to the show they want to see at one theater—but determined to see something, anything—will walk to one of the other box offices on the block. On the north side of the street are two popular restaurants, **Sam's** and **Barrymore's**, which have reasonably priced food. At one time or another they have both

Frankie and Johnnie's

had the services of the inimitable Craig Dawson as their maitre d'. Dawson had the confidence of many backstage people and knew where many Broadway bodies were buried. When he was at Sam's he would stage midnight production numbers utilizing the waiters, most of whom were Broadway chorus boys.

At the end of the block is one of the oldest restaurants on Broadway, **Frankie and Johnnie's,** on the second floor. It began life as a speakeasy in 1926 and retains the rough charm of its original incarnation. At one time New York had many such steak joints, whose food and decor were geared toward a very bare-bones, masculine esthetic. This may be the last one left.

Let's walk through Shubert Alley to 44th Street, the second-busiest street in the theater district. In 1943, *Oklahoma!* opened at the St. James, down the street. Six years later, *South Pacific* opened across the street at the Majestic. *The Phantom of the Opera* has been playing here for nearly 20 years, and there's no end in sight.

Across the street are two important watering holes. **Angus McInder** has various actors, including Matthew Broderick, among its backers, and is therefore a key place for celebrity-spotting. Across from us is the most famous theatrical restaurant of all, **Sardi's.** Like many of the city's legendary restaurants, it began life as an unpretentious Italian restaurant, serving hearty Italian food. But its strategic location across from Shubert Alley made it a key place not just for tourists to spot celebrities, but for theater people to "run into" one another and initiate or conclude theatrical deals.

Its decor has remained the same for many decades: caricatures of theatrical figures adorn its walls. The only alterations occur as new caricatures are added and those of no-longer-familiar faces are moved upstairs.

While Sardi's has always been home to "movers and shakers," it has played a far more important role in the theatrical community by showing a concern for actors. If you are an actor you are entitled to order from the actor's menu, which offers the restaurant's specialties at a reduced rate. Many an actor has been the beneficiary of the Sardis' generosity. The great actress Colleen Dewhurst remembered a time

Sardi's

Carmine's

when she was extremely short of money and had to give a birthday party for her son Campbell. She already owed Vincent Sardi a great deal but asked if she could impose upon him by bringing a group of her son's friends there. Not only did he feed them, he also hired a clown for the occasion—and refused to allow her to pay for it.

Sardi's was traditionally the place where the casts assembled after opening night to wait for the word that would decide their fates. In those days the critics attended the opening night and raced out to write their reviews against tight deadlines. Now no newspaper considers theater reviews important enough to hold an edition. The reviewers attend the previews, and the press agents know their verdicts even before the opening night curtain goes up.

Carmine's, the restaurant we're passing now, is a relative newcomer here. It dates from the early '90s, but its hearty Italian food reflects age-old Broadway traditions. The portions are so big, by the way, that many patrons leave with shopping bags of leftovers, so this may not be the ideal place to go before the theater.

Osteria al Doge

Let's cross Broadway. It's hard to believe that for decades this intersection, once known as "the crossroads of the world," was considered a hopeless cesspool of porn, pimping, and drugs. The dramatic reduction in crime under Mayor Rudolph Giuliani made tourists feel safe again in New York, and the development of new stores and restaurants in the wake of that perception was astonishingly quick.

Many lament that Times Square has become a kind of updated Main Street, U.S.A. They forget that in the late 19th century this neighborhood, fairly removed from the center of the city, was a place for stables as well as markets for horse trading. In 1888, in a cheap hotel on the northeast corner of 43rd Street and Broadway, the playwright Eugene O'Neill was born.

On the other side of Broadway and Seventh Avenue, 44th Street shows the range of cuisines available in a tiny area—**Virgil's Real Barbecue**, Mexican, Chinese, and yet another Italian restaurant, though a cut above most, the **Osteria al Doge**. Toward Sixth Avenue is one of the oldest theaters on Broadway, the Belasco, named for a great showman and pioneer in realistic theatrical scenery.

Until the 1950s, Sixth Avenue was considered a seedy street, despite the fact that the Rockefellers had insisted its name be changed to Avenue of the Americas before they would build their remarkable Rockefeller Center. In the '50s, all the little enterprises that made Sixth Avenue interesting were torn down to create these mediocre skyscrapers. Only one has any distinction: the CBS Building up at 52nd Street, designed by the visionary Eero Saarinen.

Amazingly, the blocks between Fifth and Sixth Avenues have retained their old character, none more than 44th Street. It still has a number of small, cozy hotels, the most famous of which is the legendary **Algonquin**. Sometimes people forget that the Algonquin was established before the neighborhood had glamour. It was a hotel popular with theatricals, who might not have been welcome at the Plaza or, for that matter, the old Waldorf hotel at 34th Street and Fifth Avenue, where the Empire State Building now stands. Actors were not considered desirable guests. (Nor, a century ago, could they be buried in sacred ground.) The Algonquin's famous lobby had the homey quality of a boarding house, which made the actors feel at home.

One of the things that changed the character of the Algonquin was that in 1925 a magazine called the *New Yorker* set up shop in a building across the street. In its early days the *New Yorker* resembled nothing so much as a college humor magazine. It was founded and edited by a man named Harold Ross, a scrupulous editor who was famous for asking in the margin of a manuscript

4

The Algonquin Hotel

next to a mention of Moby Dick, "Is Moby Dick the man or the whale?" Many of its best-known writers in those years were humorists like the acid-tongued Dorothy Parker; S. J. Perelman, who at various times wrote plays in addition to his stylish comic sketches; and Robert Benchley, who also served a term as a theater critic, on one occasion writing, "I saw the play under adverse circumstances—the curtain was up." They mingled easily with the actors and playwrights and journalists, and thus was the Algonquin Round Table born.

The Algonquin was never snooty. For many years it was very popular with British playwrights, because their agent, Audrey Wood, lived in one of the hotels down the block. It was owned and operated for a long time by the Bodne family. Laurence Olivier was apparently a great fan of Mrs. Bodne's chicken soup.

Lest you imagine the Algonquin is mired in the past, it should be noted that Harry Connick, Jr., whose New York debut took place at the restaurant where we began our walk, Chez Josephine, appeared in the Oak Room of the Algonquin, where he got the contracts that began his recording and motion picture careers.

For many years the Algonquin was not a culinary haven. But a new management has realized the importance of a good kitchen, and the hotel's restaurants now feature classic American dishes updated to please the far savvier contemporary American palate. This seems a cozy place to end our walk. You may want to go in and have a drink or sample that old American favorite, chicken pot pie, prepared with herbs Dorothy Parker didn't even know existed.

WALK FIVE

✿

THE EAST VILLAGE

WALK FIVE: THE EAST VILLAGE

1 City Hall
2 Theater Alley
3 65 Bleecker Street
4 Old Merchant's House
5 Bouwerie Lane Theater
6 Phebe's Tavern and Grill
7 La MaMa E.T.C.
8 New York Theater Workshop
9 Hebrew Actors Club
10 St. Mark's in the Bowery
11 City Cinemas Village East
12 Cooper Union
13 The Public Theater

Downtown City Hall Area

I t is amusing to consider that in the 1960s New York was re-garded as a dying city. Huge chunks of this not-very-large is-land were considered economically defunct. The skyscrapers that made up the skyline of Lower Manhattan had not changed since before the Great Depression. Real estate in most parts of the city was extremely cheap because the unspoken assumption was that New York was headed toward bank-ruptcy. Most of the territory we will cover on this tour would have been considered derelict in the '60s and '70s. Given how bustling the neigh-borhoods are now, that is almost in-conceivable.

It is especially strange in view of the fact that, during its first few centuries, New York invariably gave visitors an impression of extraordi-nary vitality, because until the mid-dle of the 19th century there was no distinction between commercial and residential neighborhoods. The city was alive both night and day. Given that respectability mattered

Theater Alley

less in those early days, it is not surprising that places of entertain-ment, bars, and theaters were all integrated into the fabric of the growing city.

As early as 1732, Manhattan, a town whose population was be-low 10,000, was supporting two theaters. One of them was called the New Theater, which was on Nassau Street, not far from Wall Street. To call a theater the "new theater" implies that there was an old one, making it clear that New York had a theatrical life well before this new building went up.

At the end of the 18th century, another new theater was built in Park Row, across from what would shortly be the site of **City Hall**. What is significant about that building was that it was designed by several of the French architects who flocked to America after the French Revolution, suggesting that the theater, always popular, had also become prestigious. Can it be mere caprice that a street around the corner from City Hall is called **Theater Alley?**

Just as the city itself moved uptown over the course of the 19th century, the theater kept pace with it. We're going to begin this walk at the corner of Broadway and Prince Street, now a bustling

Broadway and Prince Street

neighborhood. In 1828 a show business entrepreneur named William Niblo took over what was a genteel amusement park, the Columbian Gardens, at this corner. The neighborhood was eminently respectable, counting among its residents James Fenimore Cooper, former president James Madison, and the wealthy John Jacob Astor.

In 1829 Niblo built a theater in the midst of the gardens, and for the next few decades it was one of the most popular theaters in the city. Perhaps its most famous attraction was an 1866 show called *The Black Crook*, which is often considered the first American musical comedy. *The Black Crook* was in fact an accident. A French ballet troupe was scheduled to perform at the Academy of Music, on 14th Street, when the building burned down. Clever impresarios combined musical numbers featuring the scantily clad French dancers with a drama whose plot was roughly comparable to that of the opera *Der Freischutz*. The show was a sensation, ran for 16 months, and, although its score produced no memorable numbers, continued to be revived until shortly before the Great Depression. We shall hear more about *The Black Crook* later in our tour.

When Niblo's Gardens opened, in 1829, it was considered so far from the center of town that Niblo ran stagecoaches from the Battery to transport his audience here. By the 1830s, however, things were changing rapidly.

Let's walk East on Prince so that we can see the extent of Niblo's Gardens. The back wall of its theater faced Crosby Street, and as we walk up Crosby to Bleecker Street we can keep our eye on one of New York's hidden treasures, the **Bayard-Condict Building** at

5

number 65. It has nothing to do with the theater, but it is the only New York building designed by the great Chicago architect Louis Sullivan and has the splendid ornamentation we associate with his work. We'll turn right on Bleecker, then left on Lafayette, walk up to Fourth Street, and stop in front of 29 East Fourth, which is called the **Old Merchant's House**. It was built in 1832 and reflects a new idea in New York.

In the 18th century, wealthy New Yorkers were accustomed to living in the same place where they worked. They might have farms in the country (and in the 18th and early 19th centuries Greenwich Village was considered the country—a letter from a woman who lived way downtown on William Street in 1820 stated she never went up to Greenwich Village unless she planned to stay a week). But it was considered perfectly acceptable to live above the store. By 1832, however, New York was developing a different mindset.

Crosby Street

When this house was built, it was part of an upper-class neighborhood and surrounded by houses of equal value and character. The house was preserved because the youngest daughter of the man who built it remained unmarried and lived in it until 1933. Perhaps because she had limited options, she remained here despite the fact that the neighborhood changed radically, due in no small part to its proximity to the Lower East Side. As the immigrant populations outgrew the squalid tenements in which they first settled, they pushed onto these streets.

By the 1870s, for example, the street we are approaching, the Bowery, was full of saloons and

Louis Sullivan's Bayard-Condict Building

5

Old Merchant's House

theaters. One of the most famous of the Bowery theaters was Tony Pastor's, a variety theater, at which Pastor himself first appeared in 1865. The theater, which had been built seven years earlier, held 1,400 people, which gives you an idea of the scale of show business at that time. By 1883, Pastor, now an enormously successful producer of vaudeville, had relocated his theater to 14th Street and Third Avenue, and the building he had earlier made famous became known as the People's Theater.

Many of the Bowery theaters had high-class names, like the Windsor or the Thalia. When the nearby immigrant population was largely German, they presented German plays and German opera. By the late 19th century, however, the population of the Lower East Side teemed with Russian and Polish Jews, and many of these theaters, one of which was called the Romanian Opera House, were now presenting plays in Yiddish.

By the 1880s, the Bowery had been thrown into shadow by the construction of an elevated railroad, which in the 1890s was regarded as "the crowning achievement in solving the problems of rapid transit." New theaters were built on Second Avenue, whose sunny elegance made a great contrast to the darkness and grime of the Bowery.

If we look down the Bowery one block we see the last remaining theater, the **Bouwerie Lane**, which was for decades the home of the Jean Cocteau Repertory Theater. (Originally founded to present the plays of Jean Cocteau in repertory, it branched out to revive the work of other writers as well.) Across the Bowery is **Phebe's**, a venerable restaurant known as the Sardi's of Off-Off Broadway.

The block on whose corner Phebe's stands is East Fourth Street, one of the busiest theater streets in New York. It became a hive of theatrical activity during the late '60s, when this neighborhood, still full of Eastern Europeans (though no longer Jews), was at an economic low. You can only make a building into as economically unpropitious an enterprise as a theater when there are few other options. The fact that you could turn a whole street into not-for-profit theaters says a great deal about the economic state of New York City in the late '60s and early '70s.

5

Bouwerie Lane Theater

Phebe's Tavern and Grill

The best known of these theaters is the **La MaMa Experimental Theater Club** at 74A, with an Annex at 66. La MaMa was started by Ellen Stewart in 1967 on the site of what had been, many decades earlier, the theater of the Yiddish tragedian Boris Tomashefsky, now best known as the grandfather of the great conductor Michael Tilson Thomas. La MaMa, which has played host to theater companies from all over the world, can be rented by anyone who wants to present something that appeals to Ms. Stewart's eclectic tastes.

At one point in the mid-'70s, for example, the Romanian director André Serban was presenting a trilogy of ancient Greek plays, done in an avant-garde style and language. A colleague of Ms. Stewart's had a young friend who wanted to do an autobiographical play. The colleague sensed that there might be sequels, so he told Ms. Stewart that this work too was a trilogy. It didn't start

La MaMa E.T.C.

5

out that way, but the young man who wrote and starred in it, Harvey Fierstein, eventually made it the *Torch Song Trilogy*.

Across the street is the **New York Theater Workshop**, which became famous in 1996 when a young playwright and composer, Jonathan Larson, died before the first preview of his musical, *Rent*. By chance a *New York Times* reporter had interviewed him that very night. The dramatic and sad story propelled the show to Broadway.

All the theaters on this street reflect the rebellious mentality of the late '60s, when young actors and writers disdained the bourgeois conventions that were considered basic to the theater, such as comfortable seats or a curtain. Often in these theaters you sat in bleachers, though in recent years there has been an upgrading of amenities in some of them. For many years when you went to a show at La MaMa you waited in the lobby for Ms. Stewart to arrive ringing a cowbell and announcing the event, at which point you were allowed to take your unreserved, uncomfortable seat.

As we reach the corner of Second Avenue we approach what was an entirely different world. This was the capital of the Yiddish theater, which flourished from the latter decades of the 19th century until World War II, though its influence lingered well afterward.

Its decline can be seen as a barometer of the growing acceptance of Jews into the mainstream. The actor Muni Weisenfreund, for example, got his start in the Yiddish theater during the '20s. By the early '30s he had left to pursue a career in Hollywood under the name Paul Muni. The actress Stella Adler, daughter of one of the monarchs of Second Avenue, Jacob P. Adler, after great success in her father's company joined the Group Theater in 1930. The Group was an early version of the kind of experimental theaters that grew up on East Fourth Street three decades later. Adler had a very brief career in Hollywood in the late '30s, when Paramount demanded she change her name to Ardler, which they thought sounded less Jewish. But she returned to New York during the war and began to teach acting. Her most famous student, of course, was Marlon Brando. So we can see the influence of the Yiddish theater lasted well beyond its years of glory on this street.

The Russian-born Jacob Adler was already a star both in his native land and in London when he arrived in America in 1889. And throughout his lifetime his fame was legendary. In 1911 the Tolstoy estate awarded him the first American rights to the posthumous Tolstoy play *The Living Corpse*. In the early '20s, when the Moscow Art Theater and its illustrious director Konstantin Stanislavski came to New York, Stanislavski sought out Adler to find out how he handled certain difficult parts of the leading role.

5

Adler made his New York debut at Poole's Theater at Eighth Street and Broadway. Poole's was named for John Poole, who wrote sketches for Tony Pastor. In 1891, only two years after his arrival in America, Adler took over the theater and renamed it the Union Theater. It was here that he had one of his greatest successes, Jacob Gordin's *The Yiddish King Lear*. The original, the story of a man who gives his daughters everything, only to be forsaken by them, is as close as Shakespeare came to Yiddish tragedy, but Gordin's play was a contemporary version of it.

When Jacob Adler died, his funeral was held in Kessler's Second Avenue Theater, named for another leading Yiddish actor, David Kessler. It stood on the corner of Fourth Street and held 3,000 people, and for Adler's funeral every seat was full. The body, which had lain in state at the **Hebrew Actors Club** at 31 East Seventh Street, was carried from Kessler's down Second Avenue to Houston Street. The cortege, which was said to number 100,000, turned onto Bowery and passed the People's Theater, the National Theater, and the Grand Theater, all of which Adler had filled. The Grand, which stood at the corner of Bowery and Canal, had been built for Adler in 1904 and was the first house built specifically as a Yiddish theater.

We will walk up Second Avenue, which bears few traces of its illustrious theatrical past. This is still a neighborhood that reflects the importance of Eastern European immigration. The face sculpted on the side of the building at 126 Second Avenue next to the Ukrainian National Home is that of the beloved Ukrainian poet

Tara Schevchenko, sometimes called the Byron of Ukraine.

At the corner of Tenth Street was the now sadly missed tribute to the street's culinary legacy, the Second Avenue Deli, which had a room dedicated to one of the great stars of the Yiddish musical theater, Molly Picon. Many other luminaries of the glory days of Second Avenue are commemorated on the sidewalk in front of the former restaurant.

5

Ukrainian Poet Tara Schevchenko

Sidewalk of Stars, the former Second Avenue Deli

It is interesting to note that the church across the street, **St. Mark's in the Bowery**, holds the remains of the first governor of New Amsterdam, Peter Stuyvesant. The church, the second oldest in the city (only St. Paul's is older), is built on the site of a garden chapel of Stuyvesant's vast estate, which extended all the way up to what would later be 23rd Street. During his term as governor,

5

St. Mark's in the Bowery

80

Stuyvesant tried unsuccessfully to prevent a boatload of Jewish refugees from Portuguese Brazil from landing here in 1654. It seems wonderfully ironic that his bones should rest in a neighborhood forever identified with the people he tried to keep out of the New World.

Looking up Second Avenue we see the **City Cinemas Village East** movie theater at the corner of 12th Street. During the '50s this theater was the home of the Phoenix, one of the first successful Off-Broadway institutions. The Phoenix was famous for its revivals of classical plays as well as such new works as a legendary musical called *The Golden Apple*, a retelling of the Greek myth of Jason.

The theater gained notoriety in 1969 as the place where *Oh, Calcutta!* made its debut. In 1969 the concept of a stage full of nude actors was considered astonishing. The year before, a show called *Hair* had opened at a theater we will see a little later, but its moment of nudity was very brief and in very dim light. It was still enough to cause a sensation, so the extensive, full frontal, well-lit nudity of *Oh, Calcutta!* caused an even bigger one. When the show first opened, the nudity was counterbalanced by seemingly highbrow sketches by such writers as Samuel Beckett, Sam Shepard, Leonard Melfi, and others. Some of this "window dressing" was removed when *Oh, Calcutta!* moved to the theater district uptown, where it ran for many years, toward the end playing largely to audiences of Japanese tourists. An early instance of the perils of globalization, *Oh, Calcutta!* closed when the yen declined in value.

A century ago, the Café Royale, the Sardi's of the Yiddish theater, stood across Second Avenue from what is now the movie theater. The intrigues of the Café Royale were recounted in a comedy

5

City Cinemas Village East

Site of the Astor Place Opera

Colonnade, Lafayette Street

called *Café Crown*, which had a revival in the '80s featuring Eli Wallach and Anne Jackson as Yiddish theater royalty. My hunch is that none of the pastries at Café Royale approached the sophistication of those at the Black Hound Bakery, which stands approximately where Café Royale did.

Let us now turn westward and walk past St. Mark's Place down this little-known, charming thoroughfare named Stuyvesant Street (which I suspect even the most knowledgeable New Yorker is unlikely to know) toward Astor Place. The Astor Place Opera House stood on the triangular piece of land created by Broadway, Astor Place, and Eighth Street. It went up in 1847, only 18 years after Niblo's Gardens. In those decades the city had moved rapidly uptown, and the center of fashion was just below us on Lafayette Street. (The colonnade on the west side of Lafayette is a reminder of the elegance the street once had.) Building a theater nearby seemed a good idea; after all, you wouldn't have to run stagecoaches to bring the gentry to their boxes.

In 1849 the great British tragedian William Macready was invited by the "swells" to play Macbeth at the Astor Place Opera House. In the preceding year the city's population had swollen with Irish immigrants fleeing the Great Famine. Tension between the Irish, who counted for many of the ruffians known as the Bowery Boys, and the city's English-oriented aristocrats ran high. These tensions found some expression in the rivalry between the upper-class patrons of Macready and the less patrician fans of the American Shakespeare interpreter Edwin Forrest, who was scheduled to play the Scottish king at the Broadway Theater, further downtown, on the same night.

The Bowery Boys infiltrated the opera house and created a riot when the English actor appeared. The police were called, and more than 40 people were killed before the evening was over. If the Scottish Play carries a curse with it, that might explain why the theater was only able to subsist for a few more years, until 1853, under the pall of memories of that grisly night.

Many of the sites we have discussed so far exist only in the annals of history. But the **Cooper Union**, which stands across from us, has been in existence for over 150 years, having been erected the same year the Astor Place Opera House was torn down. Cooper Union is best known as the place where a young lawyer from Springfield, Illinois was invited to speak in February 1860 by several New Yorkers who were instrumental in founding a new political party, the Republicans. The lawyer, a gifted orator, distinguished himself and became that party's first presidential candidate and ultimately one of America's greatest presidents. But that does not concern us. We

5

5

Cooper Union

are concerned with the theatrical significance of Cooper Union. It was here in 1866 that a minister delivered a speech denouncing the nudity in *The Black Crook*, which is why we include it on this walk.

Let's walk down Astor Place to the colonnade we noted earlier. As we have seen, this neighborhood was once highly desirable. John Jacob Astor, who did a great deal to develop it, established a library on this site. Shortly after the turn of the 20th century, however, the books it housed were moved uptown to form part of the monumental New York Public Library on Fifth Avenue and 42nd Street. What had been the Astor Library at 425 Lafayette Street was converted into a social agency for impoverished Jews, the Hebrew Immigrant Aid Society. By 1966, however, the building had been empty and unused for many years. The city, which had been indifferent to the destruction of Penn Station in 1963 and the old Metropolitan Opera House in 1966, was about to destroy this far less imposing institution.

A feisty producer named Joe Papp proposed turning it into a theater and acquired it from the city for $1. Papp had gained prominence by presenting free productions of Shakespeare in New York City public spaces, beginning with a little-used amphitheater on the East River. By the late '50s he was doing Shakespeare in Central Park and found himself facing off against the all-powerful Robert Moses, who counted Parks Commissioner among his varied titles and demanded that Papp charge a minimal fee to help pay for the

The Public Theater

5

85

The Public Theater

reseeding of the grass on the Great Meadow. Papp refused to compromise on the idea of free Shakespeare. Miraculously, he won the day. Not only did he present free Shakespeare but he was also able to build a theater for his productions; his victory over Goliath gained him enormous good will and power, so when he proposed turning the Astor Library into the **Public Theater** the city was easily swayed. He carved its grand interior into a series of intimate performance spaces.

Although his theater became extremely wealthy, benefiting from both public and private contributions, Papp always saw himself as David confronting various Goliaths. In his mind Broadway was a Goliath, and though the revenue he derived from moving shows to Broadway kept this theater alive, Papp continued to regard Broadway as his deadly enemy.

Certainly the fact that his theaters were able to operate outside the bounds of costly Broadway union contracts enabled him to do a lot of experimental work that would not have been feasible uptown. The most notable of the works developed here was *A Chorus Line*, the brainchild of Broadway choreographer Michael Bennett, who organized workshops in which Broadway chorus members talked about how they had become dancers. With composer Marvin Hamlisch and lyricist Ed Kleban, Bennett wove these stories into a show that moved from here to the Shubert Theater, where it ran for more than 15 years. The show returned to Broadway in 2006, where it was once again a success.

It was the establishment of the Public Theater in 1966 that led to the Renaissance on East Fourth Street, which we discussed earlier. If in the mid-'60s this was one of the few outposts this far east and this far downtown where uptown people felt comfortable, by the early 21st century this was considered "uptown" by a burgeoning population of young people gentrifying neighborhoods even farther downtown and farther east.

5

WALK SIX

❁

THE THEATRICAL
UPPER WEST SIDE

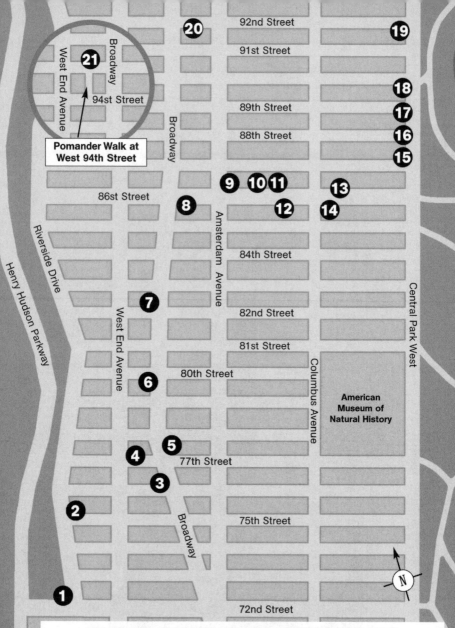

WALK SIX: THE THEATRICAL UPPER WEST SIDE

1 The Chatsworth
2 33 Riverside Drive
3 Promenade Theater
4 West End Collegiate
  Reformed Church
5 Filene's Basement
6 Zabar's
7 2315 Broadway
8 The Belnord
9 Barney Greengrass, the
  Sturgeon King
10 West-Park Presbyterian Church

11 161 West 86th Street
12 La Mirabelle
13 Hotel Cromwell
14 The White House
15 271 Central Park West
16 275 Central Park West
17 295 Central Park West
18 The El Dorado
19 The Ardsley
20 206 West 92nd Street
21 Pomander Walk

From its very inception in 1880, a project developed by the notorious Boss Tweed, Riverside Drive, which winds along the majestic Hudson River, was a street associated with status. So it's not surprising that it is also full of show business associations. We begin our tour of the theatrical West Side at the corner of 72nd Street and Riverside Drive. At the turn of the 20th century this part of the city was still considered quasi-suburban. Farther uptown were huge mansions, and it would be well into the first decade of the century before the subway would make its way that far north.

But by 1912 luxury apartment houses were going up all over the West Side, especially along West

25 Riverside Drive

End Avenue and Riverside Drive. And in the spring of that year, when Irving Berlin moved into the **Chatsworth**, 340/344 West 72nd Street at Riverside Drive, with his new bride, Dorothy Goetz, it was a sign of his extraordinary success. The building had its own

The Chatsworth

café, a hairdresser for the ladies, a barbershop for the men, a billiard parlor, and a tailor. There was also an electric bus to shuttle tenants from here to the subway, then on to Central Park.

Five months after they were married, Dorothy died of an illness variously described as pneumonia or typhoid fever. The funeral was held in their apartment, after which the body was shipped to her native Buffalo for burial.

Let's walk up to 75th Street to **33 Riverside Drive**. Its facade may be familiar as the setting for the movie *Death Wish*,

6

33 Riverside Drive

starring Charles Bronson as a man avenging the murder of his wife and children by nameless thugs. A far more important significance to the building is that in 1929 George and Ira Gershwin bought its two adjoining penthouses. Interestingly, it was the first time the boys had lived apart from their parents. At the beginning of the decade the already phenomenally successful George had bought a brownstone on 103rd Street between West End and Riverside, into which he moved his whole family. Although they had separate floors, they were in closer physical proximity than we can now imagine as comfortable, especially for someone like George, who had a reputation as a womanizer.

Their apartments a mile downtown gave the younger Gershwins a new independence. Shortly after buying their apartments, George and his older brother, Ira, who was already married, engineered a wedding for their younger sister, Frances ("Frankie"), whose beau was a young man named Leo Godowsky, son of the renowned concert pianist Leopold Godowsky. (Godowsky Sr. was also a celebrated wit. He shared a box at Carnegie Hall with the violinist Misha Elman the night of Jascha Heifetz's debut. At a certain point, Elman complained about how hot it was. Godowsky replied, "Not for pianists.")

Their mother, Rose Gershwin, by all accounts a thoroughly unpleasant, selfish woman, did not approve of the boy Frankie wanted to marry because he was not wealthy. But the boys liked him, and, more important, so did Frankie. The wedding took place here. George apparently played the wedding march with a cigar in his mouth while a rabbi that Ira found in the Yellow Pages married the young couple. Leo, by the way, turned out all right. A few years later he and a friend invented color film.

Riverside Drive remained a very chic address until World War II. After the war the West Side suffered because much of its largely middle-class population moved to the suburbs. Its buildings, most of which were constructed during the latter part of the 19th cen-

tury, languished in need of re-pair, and many were allowed to deteriorate. Their large apartments were carved into tiny dwellings, often rented at very low rates. Not until the wholesale revival of the city in the 1980s did the West Side make a startling comeback. In 1974, when *Death Wish* was made, the choice of this neigh-borhood as the site of random crime was perfect.

Let's walk toward Broadway and turn uptown. At the cor-ner of 76th Street we see across the street a theater called the **Promenade**, which was con-verted from a church in the late '70s. The theater was named for its first production, an Al Carmines musical called, of course, *Promenade*. In the lobby you can see photographs of many of the actors who have

West End Collegiate Reformed Church

appeared here, including Nancy Marchand in A.R. Gurney's *The Cocktail Hour*; William Hurt, Sigourney Weaver, and others in Da-vid Rabe's *Hurlyburly*; and a very young Kathy Bates and Bradley Whitford in a revival of Sam Shepard's *Curse of the Starving Class* in the mid-'80s.

Now head back to West End Avenue, where we come to a beau-tiful church on the corner of 77th Street, the **West End Collegiate Reformed Church**, which played a minor role in Broadway his-tory. Its minister, the Reverent Dr. Edgar Franklin Romig, in 1940 denounced the tendency, in such a time of stress, to take refuge not in religion but in a substitute he characterized as "compounded of excessive emotion, wishful thinking, and a facile evading of the rudimentary disciplines." An example of this "substitute" was what

6

Filene's Basement

Zabar's

he considered a "mawkish iteration of snatches" by the name of "God Bless America." Needless to say, in 1940 "God Bless America" and its composer found many defenders.

Look across Broadway to **Filene's Basement**, a branch of a Boston retailing institution whose greater theatrical significance we shall see shortly. Then proceed to 80th Street, where we see one of the city's most important landmarks, the delicatessen **Zabar's**. Its significance as a special kind of "Broadway show" was dramatized by the great Al Hirschfeld in a cartoon showing many of its celebrity customers in the '80s.

At 82nd Street, a few blocks above Zabar's at **2315 Broadway**, is a low building whose second floor now flies a banner for the Princeton Review, a tutoring organization that has its offices there. For many years, though, the second floor was a training ground for some of the country's best dancers. It was the home of the School of American Ballet.

As such, it embodied one of the most extraordinary stories in American cultural history. In the late '20s, a wealthy, Boston-born esthete named Lincoln Kirstein, the heir to the fortune of the founders of the aforementioned Filene's Basement, decided America ought to have a first-class ballet company. Somehow he understood that the right man to create it was a young choreographer with the Diaghilev Ballets Russes, which had been touring Europe since the Russian Revolution.

In 1933 Kirstein met the young choreographer, whose name was George Balanchine, in Paris, and proposed he come to America to create a ballet company. Balanchine responded in the affirmative and declared, "But first, a school." It would be another 15 years before the company, the New York City Ballet, would be founded, but the school was created upon Balanchine's arrival in New York in 1934, the year in which he choreographed one of his most famous ballets, *Serenade*, to the music of his compatriot Peter Ilyich Tchaikovsky.

For the next decade, the mid-'30s through the mid-'40s, Balanchine was one of the most sought-after choreographers on Broadway, creating the dances for many musicals. Among them were the 1936 Ziegfeld Follies; the 1948 *Where's Charley*, with which Frank Loesser made his Broadway debut and which starred hoofer Ray Bolger; and the 1940 Vernon Duke musical *Cabin in the Sky*, which starred Ethel Waters and dancer Katherine Dunham. His most important Broadway work was on the Rodgers and Hart shows of the '30s, like *Babes in Arms*, *The Boys from Syracuse*, and *On Your Toes*. In several of these shows, he featured his wife, ballerina Vera Zorina. His most enduring theatrical achievement, of course, was the powerful narrative ballet "Slaughter on Tenth Avenue" in *On Your Toes*. Balanchine regarded it highly enough that in 1968 he made it the only one of his Broadway ballets in the repertory of the New York City Ballet.

The Belnord

When the School of American Ballet moved to grander quarters in Lincoln Center in 1969, the studios here were taken over by a former City Ballet dancer and an excellent, demanding teacher named Richard Thomas, whose son, bearing the same name, may be familiar to you as an actor. For a while, Thomas shared the space with a Broadway dancer named Eliot Feld, who had been in the original cast of *West Side Story*. Feld left to start his own dance company. The second floor of this building served the muse Terpsichore in numerous ways. It also housed the studio of Pedro and

6

Barney Greengrass, the Sturgeon King

Olga—those were the only names on the door— who taught New Yorkers dances from south of the border.

Let's cross Broadway, walk up to 86th Street, and look at the huge block-wide building called the **Belnord** on the northeast corner. Over the years many show business people have lived in the Belnord, but perhaps the most distinguished tenant was the Nobel Prize–winning writer Isaac Bashevis Singer, whose novels were often adapted for the theater. Probably the most famous of these adaptations was his story "Yentl the Yeshiva Boy"; the 1975 play starred Tovah Feldshuh and John V. Shea and was later made into a movie musical directed by and starring Barbra Streisand. Another adaptation from a Singer story was *Teibele and Her Demon*, which appeared on Broadway in 1979 starring F. Murray Abraham, who later won an Oscar for his portrayal of Salieri in the movie version of Peter Shaffer's *Amadeus*. Singer is not exactly a show business figure, but among those who have lived at the Belnord was Zero Mostel, still best remembered as the original Tevye in *Fiddler on the Roof*.

Let's walk east toward Amsterdam Avenue. Looking across and up the street, you see a delicatessen called **Barney Greengrass, the Sturgeon King.** Barney Greengrass is itself a West Side landmark. Lines stretch well down the street on Sunday morning to get one of the few tables inside for brunch. It is of sociological interest that until the early '80s the longer line on Sunday mornings was to

6

94

buy food to take home. But starting in the '80s fewer people were eating at home, so the takeout line is now much shorter. (Kitchens in newer apartment buildings in New York tend to be tiny compared to those in pre-war buildings on the assumption that people these days are too busy to cook.)

A poignant fact associated with Barney Greengrass is that during the late '30s a regular in the Sunday line to buy smoked salmon and bagels to take out was the distinguished actor John Barrymore, whose alcoholism had soured his career. At the time he was living with the family of his Jewish girlfriend on 86th Street near Riverside Drive, and for some reason the actor whose Hamlet had been praised by no less a critic than George Bernard Shaw was dispatched on Sunday mornings to get the fixings for brunch.

West-Park Presbyterian Church

Let's walk along the uptown side of the street. The beautiful Neo-Romanesque **West-Park Presbyterian Church**, at 165 West 86th Street, has played host to various theater groups. One of them, the Riverside Shakespeare Company, presented Austin Pendleton as Richard III as well as a rare revival of the Nahum Tate adaptation of *King Lear*, the 18th-century version of Shakespeare's play that has a happy ending.

From 1911 on at **number 161,** in the first building next to the church, you might have noticed on the ground floor the offices of Dr. Abraham Rodgers, a general practitioner. In an apartment on another floor, Dr. Rodgers's young son Richard grew up. He went to elementary school around the corner on 89th Street, and in 2003, with the encouragement of his family, who also donated funds for musical education programs there, it was named for him. Like Gershwin, Rodgers was a legendary womanizer who lived with his family until a relatively late age. In 1929, when he was 27, he married Dorothy Feiner, who was a well-regarded interior designer, author of a best-selling book about design, and the inventor of the Johnny-Mop.

6

Also at this address for many years lived the eminent Broadway orchestrator Hans Spialek, who orchestrated many of the musicals of the '30s and '40s, including the aforementioned *On Your Toes*. His orchestrations were reconstructed for the show's revival under the supervision of its original director, George Abbott, in the spring of 1983. While the show was in rehearsal, its star, the Soviet-trained defector Natalia Makarova, went to visit Balanchine in the hospital to keep him abreast of what was happening during what turned out to be his final illness.

Because this is a neighborhood in which many theatrical people live, you can often see them at the cozy French bistro, **La Mirabelle**, across the street at 102 West 86th Street, which serves the old-fashioned dishes that are increasingly hard to find. It used to be closer to Riverside Drive but has been part of the West Side for several decades, something of a record in the restaurant business, where places go in and out of business with alarming speed.

La Mirabelle restaurant

Let's walk across Columbus Avenue. In the late '60s the building next to the coffee shop was an art gallery that had one of the first exhibitions of pornographic art. It's now a bank. That tells you something about how the neighborhood has changed. We're now passing the **Hotel Cromwell**. During the run of a Neil Simon comedy called *Sunday in New York*, the young actor who starred in it lived here. He didn't stay long. His name is Robert Redford, and he now has a home on Fifth Avenue. So you see, sometimes show business pays handsomely.

The White House

6

The building at the corner, the **White House**, was once the home of playwright and screenwriter Paddy Chayefsky. He is best known for his movies, like *Marty* and *Network*, but he also wrote a powerful play called *The Tenth Man*. He became so disillusioned by Broadway that his last play, *The Latent Heterosexual*, was published in *Esquire* so people could become acquainted with it, but he refused to allow it to be produced in New York. Another sign of how the neighborhood has changed is that Chayefsky and his wife bought a large apartment here in the mid-'50s after *Marty* was sold to Hollywood. They paid $50,000, which wasn't peanuts but was hardly extravagant. When Chayefsky's widow died in 2000, the apartment sold for $4 million. A curiosity is that the wall above their marriage bed still bore a remnant of a bitter argument from the mid-'60s, in the form of a huge stain from the coffee one of the Chayefskys threw at the other. Somehow in more than three decades it was never painted over.

Turning up Central Park West, we come to **number 271**. Thirty years ago, this was the home of Joel Grey, who is known, among other things, for his electrifying performance as the emcee in Kander and Ebb's *Cabaret* and for his actress daughter Jennifer, whom he used to take across the street to Central Park when she was a little girl. For a few years this building was also the home of Robin Williams, who lived in the penthouse. He moved out when the co-op board refused to allow him to buy a second apartment. Also, briefly, Meryl Streep lived here.

In the '50s, Burl Ives, who starred in the original cast of Tennessee Williams's *Cat on a Hot Tin Roof*, lived at **number 275**. For many years the same building was the home of the distinguished producer Kermit Bloomgarden, among whose credits are Arthur Miller's *Death of a Salesman*, Meredith Willson's *The Music Man*, and the most legendary of Stephen Sondheim's musicals, *Anyone Can Whistle*. (The last of these ran on Broadway for a week in the spring of 1964, but it has been observed that if all the people who claim to have seen it actually had it would still be running.) Playwright Murray Schisgal, who wrote the comedy *Luv* and was one of the screenwriters for *Tootsie*, lives here. So, for many years, did the London theater and film critic Penelope Gilliatt, who also wrote the screenplay for John Schlesinger's film *Sunday Bloody Sunday*. She was briefly married to the playwright John Osborne. During the '80s, 275 Central Park West was home to actor and future governor Arnold Schwarzenegger and his wife Maria Shriver. During part of that time, they sublet their apartment overlooking the park to rock star Rex Smith, who appeared on Broadway with Linda Ronstadt and Kevin Kline in *The Pirates of Penzance*.

6

The El Dorado

Until 1989 the north corner of 88th Street was occupied by a progressive high school called Walden. Among its alumni were two classmates and good friends, the actor Matthew Broderick and the playwright and screenwriter Kenneth Lonergan.

Here at **number 295**, one of the oldest and most distinctive buildings on Central Park West, a longtime resident was *60 Minutes* reporter Ed Bradley. Among the newer residents are two actors who began their careers in the theater but have spent most of their time in Hollywood: Kevin Bacon and Kyra Sedgwick.

The charming red brick Victorian across 89th Street was often the New York residence of the great British actor John Gielgud. Another of its tenants was one of the true geniuses of the Broadway theater, set designer Boris Aronson, who won Tony Award after Tony Award for his work on several of the Hal Prince–Stephen Sondheim musicals and is probably best remembered for his Chagall-esque vision of the town of Anatevka in *Fiddler on the Roof.*

The glamorous building on the next corner, the **El Dorado**, has been home to many Hollywood stars, among them Alec Baldwin, who has appeared on Broadway several times in recent years, in revivals of *A Streetcar Named Desire* and *Twentieth Century.* Greta Garbo's doctor lived in this building. Among his other clients was Jacqueline Onassis. Perhaps the El Dorado's most notable tenant was Nobel Prize–winning novelist Sinclair Lewis.

At the corner of 92nd Street is the **Ardsley**, whose most famous tenant for many years was Barbra Streisand. The young Streisand, despite her enormous success in the stage version of *Funny Girl,* had great difficulty finding an apartment. In the '60s her ethnic background was not an asset on the East Side. Even on the West Side, her mode of employment was not always congenial to co-op boards.

6

The Ardsley

The most notable tenant in the Ardsley was not an actress but Richard Rodgers's earliest collaborator, Lorenz Hart. Hart had a duplex at the top of the Ardsley, one floor of which he gave to his mother. Her presence on the floor below did not prevent him from throwing virtually nightly parties. Because Hart was a helpless alcoholic, Rodgers sometimes had to lock him in a room with a melody and force him to write the lyric. Genius that he was, Hart invariably solved the problem without much sweat. And no one who knows his work—such songs as "My Funny Valentine," "It Never Entered My Mind," or "My Romance"—would ever claim that the circumstances of their composition in any way compromised the extraordinary quality of his lyrics.

As Hart's health deteriorated, it was harder and harder to get him to work, though Rodgers never stopped trying. In 1942 Rodgers was approached by the Theater Guild to make a musical of one of their hit plays from the '30s, Lynn Riggs's *Green Grow the Lilacs*. Rodgers was considering working with Oscar Hammerstein, but he offered the project to Hart, who thought it too homespun for his kind of lyrics. He encouraged his partner of 25 years to work with Hammerstein. Looking across at Rodgers, he said, "Frankly, I don't know how you've put up with me all these years."

Rodgers gave him another chance, reviving their '20s hit, *Connecticut Yankee*, which had the standard "Thou Swell." Hart wrote one of his most brilliant lyrics for the revival, "To Keep My Love Alive." But his drinking and obstreperous behavior were so out of control that he had to be escorted out of the opening night performance. Three weeks later he died.

Officially, this walk ends here, but if you have a little time you may enjoy walking along 92nd Street across to Broadway. As you do, take note of the building at **number 206**, between Broadway and Amsterdam. It was here that a very young Jerome Kern lived while he was composing such songs as "They'll Never Believe Me" for Broadway. When you reach Broadway, turn uptown to 94th Street. Halfway between Broadway and West End Avenue, if you stay on the uptown side of the street, you'll see a locked gate, leading into a tiny thoroughfare that runs, parallel to Broadway, from 94th to 95th Street.

It is called **Pomander Walk** and was built in 1921. It has the same name as a hugely successful Broadway show of that period, and its building facades, which don't seem full size, are an imitation of the sets in that play. You generally don't have to wait very long for a resident to unlock the gate on the way in or out. Often he or she will let you in to walk along this unbelievably charming little private street. Not only do many current residents appear to be theater people, but among its early tenants were the Gish sisters, Rosalind Russell, and Humphrey Bogart. Pomander Walk is an exceptional reminder of the way the theater is woven into the fabric of this city.

Pomander Walk

6

WALK SEVEN

❁

THE WEST VILLAGE

WALK SEVEN: THE WEST VILLAGE

1 Sullivan Street Playhouse
2 159 Bleecker Street
3 5 Sheridan Square
4 Washington Square Park
5 1 and 2 Washington Square North
6 3 Washington Square North
7 Elmer Holmes Bobst Library
8 Judson Memorial Church
9 Provincetown Playhouse
10 38 Washington Square South
11 Minetta Tavern

12 Washington Square United Methodist Church
13 18 West Eighth Street
14 10 West Eighth Street
15 14 West Tenth Street
16 28 West Tenth Street
17 Jefferson Market Library
18 14 Gay Street
19 Stonewall Bar
20 Garage
21 Lucille Lortel Theater
22 Cherry Lane Theater
23 75 1/2 Bedford Street

In our tour of the Lower East Side we saw how New York theater history was shaped by the waves of immigrants who arrived on these shores throughout the 19th century. On this tour, which wends through the Lower West Side, we will see how our theater has been affected by another set of immigrants in the late 19th and early 20th centuries. These émigrés came not from Europe or Asia but rather from the hinterlands of America. They were refugees from a tyrant who could be as cruel as those of the Old World, though her torments tended to be psychological rather than physical. I speak, of course, of Mrs. Grundy, a stern and demanding figure who used to hold sway throughout much of the Middle West. By the 1960s her dominion had ended, but her power had been undeniable for at least a century. Rather than become her slaves, many hinterlanders took refuge in the neighborhood we shall now traverse.

We shall start here at 181 Sullivan Street, the **Sullivan Street Playhouse**, which for 42 years played host to a musical by two refugees from Texas, Tom Jones and Harvey Schmidt. The musical was, of course, *The Fantasticks*, which opened in the spring of 1960 with a cast that featured Jerry Orbach and earned pleasant if not enthusiastic reviews. But because of the passion of its producer, Lore Noto, it eventually set the record for the longest-running Off-Broadway musical. The show foundered early in its run, but Noto had the happy idea of taking it to the Hamptons in the summer of 1960. Many show business people summered there. They loved it and created a buzz when it came back to New York that fall.

The songs in *The Fantasticks*, like "Try to Remember" and "Soon It's Gonna Rain," are so familiar it's hard to realize that when the show opened it was considered experimental theater. One of the things that enabled the show to run so long was that, in contrast to the musicals opening uptown in those days, it had virtually no scenery. Instead, it called on the audience's imagination. Its low overhead, of course, was one of the things that enabled it to survive for 42 years. But in 2002, as Manhattan real estate grew in value, the site was purchased. At the time there was talk that the lower floor of the building would be converted into a restaurant, a far more lucrative venture than a playhouse.

But *The Fantasticks* couldn't stay away for long. In 2006 it returned to New York in a new Off-Broadway house, the Snapple Theater Center at 50th and Broadway.

The Fantasticks was the brainchild of two men who met at the University of Texas. Among their classmates there were Fess Parker, who starred as Davy Crockett in the Disney TV series in the mid-'50s, and Robert Benton, who cowrote the screenplay for *Bonnie*

and Clyde and then became the director of such films as *Places in the Heart* and *Kramer vs Kramer.* Another of their contemporaries was a young woman who wrote the gossip column for the student newspaper, whose name was Liz Smith.

Jones wrote the book and lyrics for the show, which was based on a play by Edmond Rostand, better known as the author of *Cyrano de Bergerac.* Schmidt first found employment in New York as an illustrator and art director, doing both for what was then the most sophisticated magazine in America, *Esquire.* In 1959 he and Benton did an article for that magazine on In and Out, by which they meant Hot or Cold, meanings those innocent words did not have 50 years ago but have had ever since.

After the success of *The Fantasticks*, Jones and Schmidt went on to write such shows as *110 in the Shade*, a musical version of *The Rainmaker*, and *I Do, I Do*, a musical version of *The Fourposter*, a Broadway play from the '50s with Hume Cronyn and Jessica Tandy. The musical starred Robert Preston and Mary Martin.

This address, 181 Sullivan Street, has another significant association. On this site in the Roaring '20s stood a speakeasy called Jimmy Kelly's. For many years before that it was a saloon, and during the early years of the 20th century a kid from the streets of the Lower East Side worked there as a singing waiter. By 1923 he had achieved considerable success as a songwriter, and one night, for nostalgia's sake, he decided to visit one of the places where he got his start.

In the '20s, Jimmy Kelly's was a place for the uptown "smart set" to go for adventure. The night he dropped in, one of the younger women there caught his eye. Her name was Ellin MacKay, and her father was one of the wealthiest men on Wall Street. The songwriter was named Irving Berlin, and here began one of the great romances of the era. Her father was adamant that she drop the lower-class Jew, but she loved him and, though her father disowned her, she married him. Her family had nothing to do with her—until the stock market crashed and Berlin gave his old antagonist $1 million to save him from financial hardship.

Let's walk up Sullivan to Bleecker Street. The apartment building at **number 159** was for many years the second home of Circle in the Square, one of the early forces in the Off-Broadway theater movement that gained ground in the 1950s. Its first home in Manhattan was at **5 Sheridan Square**. (The building no longer exists.) The theater was built in a space that had been a nightclub. In the '50s a theater in which the audience surrounded the stage on at least three if not four sides was considered a groundbreaking innovation. Throughout the '50s an effort was made to break

7

down the sense of distance between the audience and the stage. It is hard to imagine now, but in the '50s even as simple a thing as having the curtain already up in a proscenium theater was regarded as "daring."

One of the productions that put Circle in the Square on the map was a revival of Eugene O'Neill's *The Iceman Cometh* with a young actor named Jason Robards in 1956. When the play had been done on Broadway a decade earlier, the wise critic Stark Young complained about the casting. He said he couldn't really judge the play because the actors were not up to its demands. That could not

be said of the group that surrounded Robards. This was also a case where the theater itself, in which the audience surrounded the actors, contributed immensely to the play. The audience did not see the denizens of Harry Hope's bar as "up there" beyond the proscenium. The audience was, for all intents and purposes, part of Harry Hope's bar.

Two actors who met while auditioning at Circle in the Square in the '50s were George C. Scott and Colleen Dewhurst, both young and unknown. Both remained loyal to the institution. In 1975 Scott directed a production of *Death of a Salesman* with himself as Willy Loman at Circle in the Square, but by then it had moved uptown to the theater district. Among the other

1 Washington Square North

productions he did for Circle was a revival of Noel Coward's *Present Laughter*, which introduced a young actor named Nathan Lane.

Although most of the productions associated with Circle in the Square were revivals, most often of American plays, they also included new plays. One that created a sensation in 1960 was *The Balcony*, by the then little-known and controversial French playwright Jean Genet.

Let's continue walking up Sullivan to **Washington Square Park**, which was originally marshland. In the 18th century and the early decades of the 19th century it served as a potter's field, meaning a dumping ground for people whose survivors did not have the means to bury them in more respectable ground. Washington Square, being a considerable distance from the center of town throughout the 18th century, was also the site of public hangings.

It is ironic to think that by the middle of the 19th century it was one of the most fashionable addresses in New York. Among those who lived and worked at **1 Washington Square North** were Henry James, Edith Wharton, and William Dean Howells. The artists Edward Hopper and Rockwell Kent lived at number 3. James set a novella called *Washington Square* here, which was turned into an extremely successful Broadway play, *The Heiress*, in 1946 by Augustus and Ruth Goetz. (A few years later it was filmed with Olivia de Havilland and Montgomery Clift.)

Although the uptown side of the square retained its gentility much longer, the southern end had already become shabby by the turn of the 20th century. So it is not surprising that it has many theatrical associations. Let's cross into the square and look back across the street. We are facing the prisonlike **Elmer Holmes Bobst Library**, part of New York University. It was the only completed part of a plan architect Philip Johnson developed for the university that would have filled the neighborhood with comparable, hulking structures. Happily, the university did not have enough money to fulfill the plan.

Where the Bobst Library now stands, there was a makeshift theater in the early '60s. Called the ANTA Washington Square, it was a temporary home for Lincoln Center Theater, while the Vivian Beaumont was still under construction. In 1964 this temporary structure housed the original production of Arthur Miller's *After the Fall*, a play generally thought to be his retributive meditation on his relationship with his former wife Marilyn Monroe.

Even more notable was a musical that opened in the theater in 1965. Like *The Fantasticks*, and in keeping with the spirit of the neighborhood, it too called on the audience to exercise its imagination. It was a musical set in a 16th-century prison where a Spanish writer named Miguel de Cervantes described to his fellow inmates a novel he was writing about an elderly gentleman intoxicated with chivalric romances and determined to follow a career as a knight errant. The musical was called *Man of La Mancha*. Its best-known song is "The Impossible Dream."

Dale Wasserman, who wrote the book for *La Mancha*, said the ANTA Washington Square might more accurately be called a shed than a theater. It had no proscenium, no fly space, no real wings, nor any place under the stage where actors could make crosses without being seen. When they began digging tunnels under the stage for that purpose they discovered bodies later determined to be victims of the Plague of 1798. Worse, the shed had a tin roof that rattled when there was heavy rain, necessitating the management to beg the audience's indulgence while the performance paused until the

7

Judson Memorial Church

noise stopped. All of which makes the huge success of *Man of La Mancha* even more miraculous.

As we walk west we pass **Judson Memorial Church**, whose tower was designed by the distinguished architect Stanford White. In the '60s many experimental plays, notably the musicals of minister Al Carmines, were presented at Judson.

The western edge of Washington Square is MacDougal Street, and if you look down it you will see an unprepossessing marquee that reads **Provincetown Playhouse**. It has a tiny interior, but its impact on American theater has been enormous. The theater is a perfect example of how the Village created culture from the aspirations of its refugees from Middle America.

MacDougal Street

In the early part of the 20th century there stood next to what is now the Playhouse something called the Liberal Club, which was an intellectual center that occasionally presented amateur theatricals, mostly satiric and lighthearted. Sometimes, though, the plays were more serious, as we must assume were those of John Reed,

Provincetown Playhouse

who was later famous for his eyewitness account of the Russian Revolution, *Ten Days That Shook the World*. Reed was the subject of Warren Beatty's movie *Reds*.

In the basement under the Liberal Club was a restaurant called Polly's, which was run by Polly Holliday, an émigré from Evanston, Illinois, the headquarters of the Women's Christian Temperance Union. Among her customers were some recent arrivals from Iowa: George Cram Cook and his wife, Susan Glaspell. Inspired by the amateur theatricals at the Liberal Club, they decided to write and produce plays in Provincetown, Massachusetts, where they spent their summers in the mid-teens. At first they presented their plays on a porch. Next they created a theater from an abandoned Provincetown wharf. Their second summer they welcomed a refugee from the Village, Eugene O'Neill, who arrived with "a trunkful of plays."

O'Neill, of course, was by no means a hinterlander. He had been born in 1888 in a hotel in what was then Longacre Square, a neighborhood for horse trading, which later became Times Square. The Barrett House hotel, at Broadway and 43rd Street, later became the site of an office building, 1500 Broadway, that now bears an O'Neill commemorative plaque.

O'Neill's father had been an enormously successful actor who crisscrossed the country starring in *The Count of Monte Cristo*. His son did not want to imitate the commercial pap that had made his father a huge star (though, many years later, a critic listening to the highfalutin language of *Mourning Becomes Electra* was reminded of the senior O'Neill's swashbuckling success.)

His one-act plays, some based on his experiences when he ran away to sea, made a great impact in Provincetown. When they returned to New York, Cook and his wife rented the stable next to the Liberal Club. They put in hard benches, called it the Playwright's Theater, and started presenting O'Neill's plays. (For a while O'Neill lived at 38 Washington Square South.)

Among the other writers whose work they presented in the teens and '20s were many who are better known for their fiction, like Sherwood Anderson, Theodore Dreiser, and Edna Ferber. In keeping with their literary pretensions, they presented plays by such poets as Djuna Barnes, e.e. cummings, and Edna St. Vincent Millay. Glaspell herself enjoyed great success as a playwright, both here and uptown. John Reed had plays performed here, as did Edmund Wilson and Stark Young.

The Provincetown Playhouse was also a pioneer in the use of African-American actors, like Paul Robeson, Charles Gilpin, and Jules Bledsoe. There is in fact a long and distinguished history of African-American theater in New York, but the Provincetown Playhouse was one of the first places where such actors appeared in plays for predominantly white audiences.

If we walk down MacDougal Street we see a landscape that has changed little in the last 50 years. That is because Greenwich Village is a designated landmark district, which severely limits the kind of development that can take place here. Otherwise these tiny stores and cafés and theaters would have been razed long ago to make room for high-rise apartment buildings where the only businesses that could afford the rent on the ground floor would be banks and dry cleaners. But as long as the landmark law remains in effect, Greenwich Village will be the one area in Manhattan that preserves a human scale. That also explains why in this tiny stretch there are so many theaters. Often they are dark. Nevertheless they live, so to speak, in hope.

On the stretch of MacDougal below Washington Square you will note the **Minetta Tavern**, where O'Neill used to hang out—there is a mural inside the back room in which he is depicted giving notes to actors at the Provincetown Playhouse. In an apartment on this block lived Louise Bryant, the liberated woman whose favors he shared with revolutionary John Reed. (She was played by Diane Keaton in Warren Beatty's film *Reds.*)

Let's retrace our steps back up MacDougal Street. The **Washington Square United Methodist Church** at 135 West Fourth

**Washington Square
United Methodist Church**

Street was the original home of *Tony and Tina's Wedding*. Devised by an Off-Off-Broadway group called Artificial Intelligence, this piece was created to run on three weekends. The wedding itself took place in this deconsecrated church, and the reception was a mile or so away at a Puerto Rican reception hall on the second floor of a building on Third Avenue and 14th Street. But the production was such a huge success that it eventually moved uptown to the theater district, where the ceremony took place in the basement of a church and the reception in a seldom-used banquet room in a nearby restaurant.

As we walk along the western edge of Washington Square Park, it seems worth remembering that Robert Moses, who is a footnote in New York theater history for his attempt to prevent Joe Papp from presenting free Shakespeare in Central Park, fought another battle on this turf in the '50s. Curiously, Moses never learned to drive but was determined to make New York hospitable to cars, even if it meant destroying the fabric of the city. He wanted to run a highway through this square. A group of Villagers fought him and preserved this great oasis.

Across from the northwest corner of the square stands a charmless apartment building that was the home for many years of the great acting teacher Uta Hagen at 27 Washington Square North. Rip Torn was one of her neighbors. So was an actor named James Broderick, who is now best remembered as the father of Matthew. Little Matthew played on the floor when his parents made their frequent visits to Uta and her husband and fellow acting teacher, Herbert Berghof, who had been a great matinée idol in his native Vienna. Because Matthew and Uta had known each other so long it seemed natural in the late '90s for him to play Nick in a staged reading of the play in which Uta had achieved one of her great triumphs, Edward Albee's *Who's Afraid of Virginia Woolf?*

Let's walk up to Eighth Street, which was once the very heart of the Village, with several great bookstores, unusually fine re-

7

110

cord stores, and innovative clothing stores, when the Village offered alternatives to the conventional clothes in the uptown department stores. The sad realities of New York real estate have destroyed the diversity of Eighth Street. Now most of the stores sell shoes, cheap clothes, fast food, and souvenirs. In the 19th century this was still a residential street.

In 1920 Howard Dietz, who would later write songs with composer Arthur Schwartz and would also head the publicity department at MGM, lived in an apartment in a building at **number 18**. Sometimes he and his wife noticed that on Saturday nights their chandelier shook from the noise in the apartment above. One night, Dietz recalled

27 Washington Square North

many years later, just before going to the theater, he decided to go and see what was going on in the apartment upstairs. About 40 people were sitting in the living room listening to the piano improvisations of a young man named George Gershwin. Dietz found it hard to tear himself away, and soon his wife joined him. They never made it to the theater, but became regulars on Saturday nights.

For much of the 19th century, Fifth Avenue, which we're now approaching, was considered the most desirable address in New York. That continued to be the case through the early decades of the 20th century, though the chic neighborhoods were increasingly farther uptown. By the turn of the 20th century this neighborhood was already déclassé, which is why it was a suitable place for a wealthy widow named Gertrude Whitney, who was herself a sculptress and had an interest in all the arts, to have a studio here at **number 10 West Eighth**. Eventually she turned it into a gallery, which was the kernel of the Whitney Museum of American Art.

On the northeast corner of Fifth Avenue and Ninth Street once stood a decaying mansion on one floor of which lived a wealthy refugee from Buffalo named Mabel Dodge. After many years of living in Europe, absorbing advanced ideas and becoming acquainted with modern art through her friend Gertrude Stein, she returned to bring these innovations to New York with the intention of "dynamiting" the city intellectually.

7

111

Among the visitors to Mrs. Dodge's house were such revolutionaries as John Reed, Margaret Sanger, and Emma Goldman, the artists Marsden Hartley and John Marin, and A. A. Brill, who translated the works of yet another revolutionary, Sigmund Freud, into English. Reed's friend Eugene O'Neill was also a frequent guest of Mrs. Dodge. So was Reed's college roommate, Robert Edmond Jones, who became one of the most important set designers in the

10 West Eighth Street

American theater. Mrs. Dodge spread her money around liberally. Among her benefactions was a project by the radical dancer and choreographer Isadora Duncan to teach dance to children in the slums of the Lower East Side. Eventually Mrs. Dodge married a Native American, Tony Luhan, and moved to Taos, New Mexico.

Let's walk up to Tenth Street and turn west. Here at **number 14** we see the house of Mark Twain, who also dabbled in show business, giving the readings of his work that the actor Hal Holbrooke recreated throughout his long and distinguished theatrical career. Dashiell Hammett, who wrote the novel on which the film *The Maltese Falcon* was based, lived at **number 28** in the '50s. At the corner of Tenth Street and Sixth Avenue stands the **Jefferson Market Library**. The building, originally a courthouse, was slated for demolition in the '60s, but neighborhood activists fought to save it and created a new use for it as a part of the public library system.

The '60s saw the demolition of two New York City architectural treasures, the old Metropolitan Opera House and Pennsylvania Station. The realization that no building, however beloved, as in the case of the opera house, or distinguished, as in the case of the railroad station, was safe from the wreckers' ball led to the establishment of the Landmarks Law, which protected the city's extraordinary cultural heritage. At the time, Victorian architecture

14 West Tenth Street

28 West Tenth Street

such as this courthouse was totally out of fashion, and those who opposed the establishment of the landmarks law were aghast. As one of them put it, if they save this, they'll save anything. Fashions, happily, change, and now we see the charm and grace of a building like this and realize what a huge loss its destruction would have been.

Jefferson Market Library

14 Gay Street

As we follow Tenth Street toward Greenwich Avenue, we come to the part of the Village that was always Bohemian, unlike the blocks off Fifth Avenue, which were once patrician. Behind the Jefferson Market Library is a sweet park on the site of what was for many years the Women's House of Detention. The building itself, despite its function, had an odd Art Deco charm. It also provided street theater, as the male and female lovers of the inmates shouted greetings to their incarcerated beloveds.

Let's turn left onto Christopher Street, the first street beyond Sixth Avenue. Then, very quickly, we make another left onto Gay Street, named in the 19th century when the adjective implied no more than cheerfulness. At **number 14**, one of the buildings painted white, Ruth Sherwood and her sister Eileen lived when they came to New York from Ohio to seek fame and fortune. Gay Street runs between Christopher and Waverly Place. So it's not surprising that in the first song in *Wonderful Town*, by Betty Comden, Adolph Green, and Leonard Bernstein, based on the comedy *My Sister Eileen*, a tour guide singing the praises of Greenwich Village mentions both streets to his group of tourists.

Let's walk along Waverly toward Seventh Avenue. Across the triangle on Christopher Street is the **Stonewall Bar**, which became famous in June 1969, the night of Judy Garland's funeral, when the Stonewall's gay clientele got into fisticuffs with police, leading to the birth of the gay liberation movement.

We'll cross over to the island with the subway entrance and look back at the restaurant called **Garage**. During the '70s and '80s Garage was the home of Circle Rep, the company that presented the works of Lanford Wilson and discovered the brilliant set designer John Lee Beatty and the actor Jeff Daniels.

Stonewall Bar

Garage

Lucille Lortel Theater

As we cross Seventh Avenue, look uptown. Although you can't see it, Times Square is exactly a mile and a half away, but the atmosphere of the Village is such that it might just as well be in some other city.

Let's walk along Christopher Street until we come to the **Lucille Lortel Theater**, in front of which is a sidewalk of stars who performed in what may be the most famous of Off-Broadway theaters. Until 1952 this was the site of a rundown movie house. In that year a not-very-skillful producer named William DeLys bought it and turned it into a legitimate theater. It was going to be run along the lines of the "club" theaters in London, which, because of their quasi-private status, were able to present more daring fare than public theaters, which remained under government censorship for much of the 20th century.

When the Theater de Lys opened in September of 1952, its first production was a musical version of a play the film director John Houston had written 24 years earlier based on the legend of "Frankie and Johnnie." It was a catastrophe, and DeLys immediately skipped town. In 1954 the theater was bought by a man named Lou Schweitzer, whose grandfather had invented a chemical that retarded flames and was used in the manufacture of cigarette paper. Schweitzer bought it for his wife, the former silent screen actress Lucille Lortel. A few days after he acquired it, its most legendary success opened: an adaptation of Kurt Weill and Bertolt Brecht's *The Threepenny Opera*, which ran for nearly six years.

116

Cherry Lane Theater

Edna St. Vincent Millay's house

In 1980 Lortel, by then an enormously wealthy widow, renamed the theater for herself, which was fair, considering she had run it infinitely longer and with greater success than Mr. DeLys.

Let's cross Christopher Street and walk up Bedford to Commerce Street, where we'll turn right and walk toward the **Cherry Lane Theater**, one of the oldest in the Village. The building began its life as a silo early in the 19th century. Over the years it was a tobacco warehouse and a box factory. In 1924 it was turned into a theater by Edna St. Vincent Millay, who lived around the corner at **75 1/2 Bedford Street**, a building that is nine and a half feet wide. In her early years in New York, Millay wrote and acted in plays as a member of the Provincetown Players. The Village, which has always had a youthful aura, seems just the place "Let's turn this old barn into a theater" could actually happen.

⌘

ODDS AND ENDS

Al Hirschfeld's house

The preceding walks have been organized with an eye to acquainting the theater lover with sites of historic interest. The proximity of these sites to one another reflects the way the New York theater tended to grow with the city itself, largely because it has always been so intimately intertwined with the city's economy.

There are, however, several significant sites that are not close to anything else but are of great interest to anyone who cares about the theater.

One such place is the **Players** at 16 Gramercy Park South, on 20th Street between Park Avenue South and Irving Place. Although it is a private club, The Players frequently opens its doors to people who are not members. For some years, in a series called Food for Thought, the club has followed a buffet lunch with readings of plays, both famous and obscure, featuring well-known actors. Since early 2006 Project Shaw has held monthly readings of plays by Bernard Shaw, also with distinguished casts.

This unexpectedly homey Gothic Revival brownstone originally belonged to the great 19th-century actor Edwin Booth, who bequeathed it to members of his profession in order to help them mingle with "gentlemen." In Booth's time, after all, it was not always customary to permit actors to be buried in sacred ground. If the gulf between actors and gentlemen seemed much greater back then, it was certainly not helped by the actions of Booth's younger brother John Wilkes, a cogent example of why it is probably not good for actors to make political statements.

The interior has changed considerably over the years—what was formerly a garden in the back, for example, was covered and converted into a little theater. The one room that has remained exactly the same for well over a century is the bedroom where Booth died. In cases throughout the club are the costumes Booth wore in his legendary portrayals

The Players

Statue of Edwin Booth in Gramercy Park

of Shakespeare's heroes. There is a statue of the actor across the way in Gramercy Park, also a private institution. On Shakespeare's birthday, however, the park is opened to the public as festivities are held around Booth's statue. As a boy, John F. Kennedy played here when his family lived on the other side of the park in the Gramercy Park Hotel. Among those who stayed in the hotel was Humphrey Bogart, who was married there. A longtime resident of the hotel was the writer S. J. Perelman, who made a few forays into the theater, one a farce called *The Beauty Part*, which starred Bert Lahr.

The exterior of The Players is the work of the eminent turn-of-the-20th-century architect Stanford White, who designed its gracious two-story porch, its imposing wrought-iron lantern, and its beautiful iron railings.

Another noteworthy theatrical home is the charming brownstone that for many years belonged to Alfred Lunt and Lynn Fontanne at **150 East End Avenue,** just above 86th Street and right across from Carl Schurz Park (around the corner from the official residence of New York City's mayor, Gracie Mansion). The Lunts' home is not a public building, but it is of interest because of the quaint block on which it stands.

The house at the northeast corner of 86th Street and East End Avenue belonged to one John C. Henderson, who made a fortune selling fur hats. By one account he built the houses facing the park for his children, and the somewhat smaller ones behind them (on the tiny street that bears his name, Henderson Place) for their servants. According to what is probably the more reliable history, the entire set of Queen Anne buildings was built on what was hitherto farmland as a speculative venture. When the Lunts acquired their building in the '50s, the neighborhood was considered Bohemian.

The luxury apartment house that stands at the corner of 87th and East End supplanted Doctors' Hospital, which occupies a special place in New York social history. It had a well-appointed restaurant on its first floor, but visitors who wanted to dine in a patient's room would be served on a table brought to the room and fitted out with fine linen and proper silver. And those who wanted to spend the night near a patient wouldn't have to squirm on a cot; a bed in a nearby room would be made available. (Nearly all its rooms were private.)

It was not considered one of New York's better hospitals in terms of medical care, but its amenities may explain why Cole Porter went there in 1937 after the tragic accident in which a skittish horse crushed both his legs. It was also the place where the incomparable

lyricist Lorenz Hart checked himself in several times to dry out, and where he died in 1943. While they were working on *On the Town*, composer Leonard Bernstein and choreographer Jerome Robbins both required minor surgery and checked themselves into adjoining rooms here.

Let me share a personal reminiscence that sheds some light on this somewhat unorthodox medical institution, where I once spent three weeks enjoying excellent care for a serious malady. On my way to visit a patient some years later, I saw a distinguished-looking elderly doctor come through the front door. As his chauffeur opened the back door of the waiting Rolls Royce, the doctor took his stethoscope from around his neck and handed it to the driver. I found this little ritual so amusing I described it that night to someone at a party. By chance she not only knew the doctor's name but asked, "Did you happen to notice that the stethoscope was gold?"

The home of the Lunts,
150 East End Avenue

Not too far away, at **122 East 95th Street,** is the house that for many years belonged to the great chronicler of the New York theater Al Hirschfeld, whose drawings have been the most lasting images of many Broadway shows. Hirschfeld and his then wife, Dolly Haas, who had been a star in Berlin between the wars, were pioneers when they moved here in the '40s, but soon their neighbors included Betty Comden, Marlene Dietrich, and Vincent Sardi, Jr. One of the reasons they bought the house was its bust of Tri-

Al Hirschfeld's house

ton, which they thought gave it a European air. A plaque marking Hirschfeld's house as well as his contributions to the New York theater was affixed to the building in May 2006.

On the outskirts of the theater district is one of the most influential institutions in the American theater. Housed in a deconsecrated church, over the years the **Actor's Studio** has acquired a sacred aura of its own. Located at 432 West 44th Street between Ninth and Tenth Avenues, the Studio was founded in 1947, largely by former members of the Group Theater, the visionary ensemble that tried to create a purer form of theater during the Depression. Like its predecessor, the Studio was conceived as a utopian experiment, an attempt to see what actors could achieve when not hampered by the demands of the commercial theater or the vulgar needs of the audience. However hostile the Studio was to the notion of theater as a creature of the marketplace, it was unable to resist the appeal of movie stars. Though its most famous members were Lee Strasberg and Elia Kazan, it also offered an artistic haven to Marilyn Monroe. When he was a struggling unknown sharing a Lower East Side apartment with Jerome

The Actor's Studio

Ragni (who later wrote *Hair*), Dustin Hoffman auditioned to become a member of the Studio several times. He was not accepted, but after *The Graduate* made him an instant star, Hoffman was *invited* to join.

At the time of the Studio's founding, the West '40s were home to many people who worked in the nearby Broadway houses—not just actors, but crew members, bookkeepers, usherettes, and box office people. It was a small town through which theater news passed very quickly. Now, of course, virtually the only place people who work in the theater can afford to live is **Manhattan Plaza**, which spans the block between 42nd and 43rd Streets from Ninth Avenue to Tenth. During the financial crisis of the '70s, what had been built as a speculative venture was given to the city, which designated part of the huge structures as fair market housing, the rest as housing for artists based on financial need. It spurred the financial stabilization and eventually the revitalization of this neighborhood that once bore the intimidating label Hell's Kitchen.

Few New York addresses are as closely associated with the city's artistic life as the **Chelsea Hotel,** 222 West 23rd Street. The com-

Chelsea Hotel

poser and music critic Virgil Thompson lived here most of his life. Painters of the New York School such as Jackson Pollock, Willem de Kooning, and Larry Rivers stayed here. Andy Warhol shot a scene from his early three-hour epic *Chelsea Girls* here. Among its theatrical residents were Sarah Bernhardt, Eugene O'Neill, Tennessee Williams, Brendan Behan, and, after his divorce from Marilyn Monroe, Arthur Miller. Miller's 1964 autobiographical play *After the Fall* was written while he lived here.

Less well known but almost as rich in artistic history is the **Hotel Elysée,** 56-60 East 54th Street, where Tennessee Williams died in 1983. It was the favorite hotel of Tallulah Bankhead, who starred opposite Tab Hunter in his only Broadway appearance, Williams's play *The Milk Train Doesn't Stop Here*. Ethel Barrymore stayed here, and so did Lillian Hellman and Dashiell Hammett. A nontheatrical person of some note who often stayed here was Joe DiMaggio. The Elysée is the home of the Monkey Bar, a room of fanciful period charm.

New York is full of places that were the starting points for great careers. Admirers of Montgomery Clift can go to several buildings where the actor lived, but two of them can be found on the very same street. Beginning in 1951, when his movie career was going well, he had a duplex in the building at **209 East 61st Street**. In 1960 there was an extensive fire, forcing him to move, so he bought the brownstone down the block at **217 East 61st**. It was in this building that he died in 1966.

Not far away, on Third Avenue between 67th and 68th Streets, is the walkup where Barbra Streisand lived, at **1157 Third Avenue**. Part of that time she shared the apartment with her first husband, Elliott Gould. In those days the apartment was above a middling fish restaurant, Oscar's Salt of the Sea. Now the downstairs tenant, Ann Taylor, is far classier.

Katharine Hepburn used to live at 244 East 49th Street. These two blocks, 48th and 49th Streets between Second and Third Avenues, are known as **Turtle Bay**. All the residents share a charming garden in the middle. Among Hepburn's neighbors used to be Garson Kanin, the author of *Born Yesterday*, and his wife, Ruth Gordon, the star of many movies but probably best remembered for *Rosemary's Baby*. In one of their memoirs about Hollywood, which they wrote in the mid-'70s, the couple broached a subject long known but rarely mentioned in print: Hepburn's affair with

Spencer Tracy. Hepburn made her displeasure known, and the Kanins moved. Another resident of Turtle Bay is Stephen Sondheim.

On West 46th Street, number 229, stands the **Church of Scientology**, whose adherents include Tom Cruise and John Travolta. Travolta had a brief, successful Broadway career in *Grease* and *Over Here*, a musical with the Andrews Sisters, before hitting it big in TV and movies. At 227 West 46th Street, an address that has disappeared, there used to be a rooming house for vaudeville artists. At one time it was home to an aspiring vaudevillian named Archie Leach. Happily, vaudeville died, and he went to Hollywood with the name Cary Grant.

Older theater lovers may remember a time when the theater was invested with glamour. Two addresses on the East Side evoke that time—**Sutton Place** and **Beekman Place**.

In the Irving Berlin tour we noted that Berlin ended his days at 17 Beekman Place, which is in the middle of this tiny thoroughfare that runs from 49th Street to 51st along the East River. It is interesting to note that, until the '20s, Beekman Place was a slum. It was, after all, just north of the slaughteryards that occupied the space until the late '40s, when the United Nations was built.

Greta Garbo had an apartment in number 2. The famous producer Billy Rose lived at number 5, the celebrated actress Katharine Cornell and her husband, the producer/director Guthrie McClintic, lived at number 6. If you stand at the lower end of Beekman Place and face the United Nations Plaza, the luxury high-rise across the way, you're looking at Sutton Place, where Truman Capote once lived. His adaptation of his own novella *House of Flowers* was a flop in 1954, but it yielded the great Harold Arlen song "Sleeping Bee."

Sutton Place also runs along the river a few blocks uptown. In *Manhattan*, Woody Allen and Diane Keaton snuggle on a park bench on Sutton Place with a spectacular view of the Queensboro Bridge. This posh address has been the home of perhaps more "angels" than writers and performers. The development of Sutton Place was apparently encouraged by a theatrical and literary agent named Elizabeth Marbery, who was a close friend of the innovative and highly fashionable decorator Elsie de Wolfe. Their presence gave the street, which was only developed in the teens of the last century, chic.

Poised between these two streets is another glamorous address, **River House**, which overlooks the river at the end of 52nd Street at number 435 East. The great director Joshua Logan and his wife Nedda, the daughter of the vaudevillian Ned Harrigan (of Harrigan and Hart) lived here for many years.

River House

Another famous tenant was Mary Martin. Martin's husband, Richard Halliday, handled all the mundane aspects of her life. Apparently one day he was too ill to shepherd her to the theater where she was performing, and when she got into the taxi that evening she realized she didn't know where she was going. But she mentioned the name of the show, *South Pacific*, and the driver knew to take her to the Majestic.

When River House was built at the beginning of the Depression, it had a yacht dock for its residents. The dock was supposedly the inspiration for Sidney Kingsley's play *Dead End*, which dramatized what had long been a fact of life for New Yorkers—the very rich and the very poor lived together cheek by jowl. Both ends of the spectrum were discommoded by Robert Moses when he built the East River Drive, now the Franklin Delano Roosevelt Drive. The tenement kids could no longer dive from the dock, and the rich could no longer "drive home" from wherever on their boats.

Although it is frequently declared that Manhattan is now exclusively for the wealthy, the most privileged New Yorkers have nevertheless lost a few perks over the last century. What sharper image is there of the indignities they have suffered than the fact that they can no longer "park" at River House?

INDEX

Index

Index

Index

Index

Index